Seven Sisters

*Spiritual Messages
from Aboriginal Australia*

Laine Cunningham

Seven Sisters
Spiritual Messages from Aboriginal Australia

Published by Sun Dogs Creations
Changing the World One Book at a Time

ISBN: 9781946732088

Full Color, Hardcover Edition with Enhanced Content

Copyright © 2015, 2016 and 2017 Laine Cunningham

All rights reserved. No part of this book may be reproduced in any form or by any means, electronic, mechanical, digital, photocopying or recording, except for the inclusion in a review, without permission in writing from the publisher.

Praise for Seven Sisters

Winner, *Carolina Woman* Inspiration Award
Author Featured in Huffington Post, *First for Women*, *Awareness*, and *New Age Journal*

"Loved it! The traditional Aboriginal stories are fascinating reads. From reading Laine's book, it's easy to feel the sacredness in the Aboriginal culture. I hadn't felt this moved by Aboriginal spirituality since viewing Oprah Winfrey's visit to Australia's Uluru rock."

—Virginia Lathan

"Having no pre-knowledge of Aboriginal folklore, I found *Seven Sisters* to be both educational and inspiring. The fact that Laine Cunningham spent six long months on her own in the Australian outback before writing this book leant a rich authenticity to her voice as she shared from her abundantly full, and talented, heart.

"I absolutely adored this book and keep it in the top drawer of my bed table so I can go back to the Dreamtime anytime I need to be rescued from the dream killing drudgeries of this life. *Seven Sisters* is a treasure!"

—Leah Griffith, Award-winning Author, *Cosette's Tribe*

"What Laine Cunningham provides in this brief but poignant book is not only a sense of background for a refreshed knowledge of the Aborigines, but she also has written a number of essays about tribal customs and how they relate to the processes of connecting to the world - physically, through gender identity, through Dreamtime energy."

—Hall of Fame Reviewer

"Well written and highly informative, *Seven Sisters* was even better than I'd hoped."

—C Laney, Author
Lessons from the Cockpit

"Ever since Laine's first book on Australia, *The Family Made of Dust*, I have waited anxiously for her next creative work. *Seven Sisters* molded a deeper understanding of the indigenous concept of 'Dreamtime.' Laine has delicately represented a series of spiritual perspectives leading us to the core of the Aboriginal heart. With her insight, she must have been a native medicine woman in a previous life."

—Dale Stacy, Author
Diamond in the Rough

"An intriguing look at the culture of Australia told through a rich oral history and passed down through the ages. The stories they tell are their way of explaining many mysteries of the universe and of life."

—Mary Blowers, Book Review Blog

"As a teacher I can see this book being great for many audiences. I personally enjoyed the stories as a nice afternoon pleasure read. I can see the book as a whole being used with older children to help them learn to analyze text and younger children to help teach important life lessons."

—Robin Perron, Teacher

"*Seven Sisters* is comprised of unique stories that have been passed down from generation to generation among the Australian Aborigines. The stories offer insights into another culture, each with a life lesson, and the author adds her own insights to each story."

—Shaman Elizabeth,
Author with the Foundation for Shamanic Studies

"An inspirational book which is most likely to change your perspective on a lot of things. The book is the outcome of six months of solitary camping in the Australian outback, which by any means is no small feat. Through these valuable lessons, you will learn that the issues confronting humanity like environment, love, friendship, parenting and life can be resolved if one applies the unchanging wisdom of the human heart."

—Top 500 Reviewer

"As you flip through the pages of *Seven Sisters*, before you have even read a page, you can sense a special essence about the book. The design from the cover flows through the pages giving the reader a feeling of the wholeness that Laine Cunningham shares of her knowledge of Australian Aboriginal culture.

"As Cunningham concludes the book, she explains that it is her goal to assist each individual in identifying the message that is meaningful to them on their own individual journey. She defines a divine consciousness that has always resided within us personally and within all cultures. Her concluding paragraph is an affirmation of life."

—Shirley, Goodreads Reviewer

"Laine Cunningham gifts us with a collection of essays that tie into traditional Aboriginal stories, teaching us that Dreamtime Energy is a timeless energy that can address modern issues with love and relationships, friendship and community, illness and joy.

"Each of these stories stem from myths but Laine's presentation of the stories or myths proves more enlightening on how to live in peace and love for all. She is our spiritual messenger bringing us universal truths from an ancient yet extant culture. Mesmerizing and meaningful and inspiring."

—Grady Harp, Vine Voice, Hall of Fame Reviewer

"I thought this book would be a quick read, but I found myself lingering, absorbing the message of each story before moving on to the next. I found this book to be both entertaining and informative, one I will probably reread quite a few times."

—Dena Harris, Award-winning Author,
Who Moved My Mouse? A Self-Help Book for Cats

Table of Contents

DESERT DREAMING 1

SEVEN SISTERS 5

    THE MESSAGE OF SEVEN SISTERS 9

WAR 13

    THE MESSAGE OF WAR 16

THE PRANK 20

    THE MESSAGE OF THE PRANK 23

THE ORPHAN 27

    THE MESSAGE OF THE ORPHAN 30

HUNGER 34

    THE MESSAGE OF HUNGER 38

THE DANCE 42

    THE MESSAGE OF THE DANCE 45

THIRST 49

    THE MESSAGE OF THIRST 51

TRICKERY 56

    THE MESSAGE OF TRICKERY 59

YANDYING 63

    THE MESSAGE OF YANDYING 66

THE GLOW 71

The Message of The Glow	74
THE PROMISE	78
The Message of The Promise	80
A FINAL MESSAGE	84
A FREE SAMPLE FROM *WOMAN ALONE: A SIX-MONTH JOURNEY THROUGH THE AUSTRALIAN OUTBACK*	85
A FREE SAMPLE FROM *THE FAMILY MADE OF DUST*	91
ABOUT THE AUTHOR	98
OTHER WORKS BY LAINE CUNNINGHAM	99

Desert Dreaming

Some years ago, I spent six months camping alone in the Australian outback. Every night I cooked over an open fire as dingoes patrolled the bush. I heard the stories of travelers and citizens along with Aboriginal lore. The experience made me recognize new truths, some of which became clear only after I had returned to America.

One of those truths is that people haven't changed much for thousands of years. Planes and global commerce have replaced ponies and trade routes, yet still we struggle to put food on the table. The internet makes other nations our neighbors even as our careless words hurt people we love. None of our glorious technological advances have resolved the issues of the human heart.

Even changes that enhance our lives can cause trouble. The speed of progress demands ever-faster adaptations that leave some people feeling unbalanced. Extremists embrace bombs as "final solutions." The void between human rights and religious beliefs seems as large as ever. Meanwhile, the culture of celebrity buries meaningful experience beneath glittering photos and instant video feeds.

At its core, this chaos is neither bad nor good. It is only a symptom of growth. Our global society is a teenager searching for what it might become. Guidance comes from the elders, cultures that predate our multi-gig civilization. The parents of our modern age are the social and religious traditions that developed during the last few thousand years. Its grandparents are tribal and spiritual systems that are older still.

LAINE CUNNINGHAM

Throughout time and across all countries, the one constant has been our stories. Folktales told around the campfire have become movies lit by electric fire. Long ago, different versions were told to older listeners to help them tackle more complex issues. Films and books do the same by targeting youth or adults, Gen Y or boomers. As society changes, the details of our stories change. Since we are still dealing with the same challenges, though, the messages remain the same.

Our personal stories work the same way. Every time employees gather in the breakroom, they share tales from their lives. When we discuss the plot of a popular TV show, we share perspectives, teach lessons, and search for meaning. Movies, books and documentaries show us how other people think and live. Open video sites show us what we think about ourselves and how we want others to see us. On YouTube, Facebook and blog sites, we try out the roles of hero and antihero, villain and victim.

All these stories have little to do with tribes or nations and everything to do with being human. Each tale provides us with another solution to the riddle of how to be our best. We become patient with our relatives and ourselves; we forgive our enemies even when they are friends who have betrayed us. Every hero thrills by mirroring our own potential. Every villain chills by showing us the same.

Stories have always been an important part of our humanity. Our brains are hardwired to envision new lives and try out different perspectives. Our imagination spins wonderful tales while our logic registers the lessons. The process gives us a safe way to explore an unsafe world. Stories spark our greatest power, the ability to grow using only our minds.

Tales from Aboriginal Australia can transform us spiritually. Of course, the culture and geography of the Dreamtime are different than our own. Yet the messages and the essays that delve into those messages deal with everyday issues: illness and joy, victory and death, love and friendship. The original instructions were given to us all. We all seek peace within ourselves and harmony with others.

According to Australia's ancient cultures, all creatures and things emerged from the Dreamtime. The Dreaming is not just a collection of lore or a long-ago time; it is a living energy that flows constantly through the universe. It is then and now, divine and human, spirit and law. It teaches us how to survive in a harsh world and how to thrive in our souls.

Most clans conceived of a creation in which Earth already existed. Ancestors rose out of the ground and descended from the sky. Wherever their feet pushed up mounds, mountains arose; wherever the ancestors fought, the ground was trampled flat. Tribal members can still "read" the land by walking a story's path, its songline. In this way the people were connected to the land.

The largest songlines, epic stories of ancestors who ranged far across the continent, connected different tribes. When an ancestor crossed into new territory, the next part of the story belonged to the neighboring group. The entire songline could only be recited when all the tribes had gathered. Relationships between neighbors were therefore automatically—and spiritually—strengthened.

After walking those songlines myself, I returned to the United States with a very different perspective. My corporate job quickly imploded. I could no longer tolerate the gossip-ridden hallways, rules that were unevenly enforced, or that the environmental consulting firm was paid to assign monetary value to human life. And my fellow coworkers could not tolerate the negativity I had not yet purged from my soul.

I started anew as an author. As I offered the gift of Aboriginal folktales to others, messages from other cultures changed my perspective further. I started to become what I am today. I started to discover who I had been all along. My wish is that the stories in this book and the perspectives in the essays give you the same opportunity for growth, love, hope, and an abiding peace.

Walk with me now into the desert. Rocks jut out of the ground and everything is dusted in pink and red. Wiry clumps of spinifex grass sprout from the plain, and the purple flowers of bush tomatoes promise a sweet harvest. Smell the tang of eucalyptus trees and taste the cool water from a shady billabong. Hear the droning didgeridoo and the sharp click-sticks that accompany the songs. Take whichever Dreamtime messages will help you and your tribe as the gifts they are intended to be.

From the Heart of Love,
Laine Cunningham

Seven Sisters

Every Aboriginal girl looked forward to her initiation, the rites that would make her into a woman. Although the transition would be a happy time, the girls couldn't help but worry. They wondered if they would be able to learn all the songs and remember the lessons. Their bodies would know when the time had come and would make physical changes all by themselves. That knowledge gave the girls some comfort.

Boys underwent their own initiations, of course, frightening rites of blood and pain. Not every child succeeded the first time. When one boy failed the man-making ceremony, the shame was more than he could bear. To soothe his humiliation, he loudly claimed that girls were weak because their initiation wasn't nearly as difficult.

A young woman who had just completed her own rites grew angry at his words. Women's lives held dangers and pains no man could comprehend. Why, a mother had died in childbirth only the year before. Was she supposed to think less of the men because they would never face that danger? Ridiculous!

Still, the comments buzzed in her mind like a horde of bushflies. She wondered if other boys or even men thought the woman-making rite was less valuable. After fretting over this for days, she told her sisters something shocking. She was going to ask the elders to make her into a man.

The youngest sister, a reed-thin girl with hair like the floss of a kapok tree, began to cry. She thought the ceremony would actually change her sister's body into that of a man. Even after the others convinced her that wouldn't happen, she would not be silent.

The boys will say it's not fair to compare them to an adult, she said. *They must see that girls are also strong. I will go with you!*

For a long moment, no one spoke. Then it was agreed: If one went, they all went. What one suffered they would all suffer. The seven sisters had been that way ever since their mother had pushed them into the world like a living chain of years.

As they walked back to camp, they didn't say another word. Just by looking at the girls, everyone knew something serious was about to happen. Mothers put aside their grinding rocks and grandmothers scooped up the babies. Men stopped repairing their weapons, and even the boys abandoned their games to tag along. By the time the sisters stood before the elders, the entire camp had gathered.

The senior men and women knew the girls as wards to be cared for, as young minds that were curious yet lacking in experience. The oldest sister had already done much for her people so she was allowed to speak. When she did, the elders couldn't believe they had heard her correctly.

Test us with the man-making ceremony, the oldest sister said again. *Let us prove we are equal to men.*

For many hours the council discussed the request. Even as darkness grew, no one moved to light the fires or prepare food. Finally the senior woman nodded. Their request would be granted. As the oldest sister joined the ensuing celebration, she felt the eyes of the sky spirits on her. Her request was so unusual even they wanted to know if she would succeed. She could only hope that she would endure.

For the next few days, the girls' uncles disappeared for hours at a time. When they wandered back, they pretended not to have been gone while everyone else pretended not to have noticed their absence. One day the uncles left for only a short time. Then they leapt out of the bush shouting war cries.

The girls' mother and aunts grabbed the sisters in trembling arms. The men tugged and shoved, intent on breaking the sisters free. It was time to change. Separating the children from everything they had ever known was the first step.

When the oldest sister's head was covered with a dingo pelt, she plunged into a darkness she'd never known existed. Each girl would face the ordeal alone. Hands guided them roughly into a fast run and the mourning cries of their aunts fell behind. For them, the girls were already dead.

By the time they reached the bora ground, the ceremonial site, their feet were bloody from thorns and stones. A man sang a song they had never heard before then told the girls to sing. They stammered as best they could through the chant. When the pelts were finally removed, the sisters saw seeds and stones arranged to form a symbol important to men.

The evening decayed into a dark night. The uncles left. For the first time, the girls weren't surrounded by aunties who could explain every sound and warriors who could defend against every enemy. If they lit a fire to drive away their fears, they would fail. If they fled the bora ground in terror, they would fail. If they attempted to return to camp, they would shame their family.

Strangeness haunted the dark hours. Terrible howls rose out of the bush and the sound of running feet mysteriously went nowhere. A sudden snap of branches startled the girls; a rhythmic clapping like boomerangs tapping together drove thorns into their temples. None of it made sense and all of it was terrifying.

When the sun finally rose, the uncles returned looking as rested as ever. The sisters were ragged and had bunched tightly together. The men lined them up and counted; seven remained. The girls had passed the first test. They had controlled their fear.

Training began in earnest. The men recited stories and songs that spoke of a man's life, his duties and his pride. The sisters stood motionless as their lips were cut over and over with a sharp stone. The sun wheeled through its burning cycle but they were given no food. Water was offered only at dusk, and then only what could be held in the palm of a man's hand.

After days of this, the uncles brought a feast. Bush tomatoes and bush potatoes and witchetty grubs had been roasted on hot coals. The loin of a kangaroo dripped with juice and the drumsticks of a bustard let off a smoky steam. Although their stomachs ached, the sisters took only enough to sustain their lives. In times of famine, their discipline would serve the entire clan. They had passed the final test.

The uncles used the sharp stones to scratch their own arms. They gathered up their blood and sprinkled it over the initiates as they sang the last song. The sisters had become men.

As they left the bora ground—this time without the cloak of youthful ignorance—everything looked different. They had a new path in the world and saw things from a different perspective. The oldest sister had felt much the same after her initiation into the world of women. Now she saw the world with the eyes of a man and a woman.

A corroboree, a celebration, was held in their honor. The oldest sister felt joy and pride. A part of her stayed detached, though, as if her soul moved in an entirely different realm. She yearned to transform again. Before that happened, she would be with her tribe for one more night…and then forever after.

Toward dawn, the corroboree was still going strong. The sun touched the horizon, yet the stars glowed like brilliant crystals. The sun climbed higher but the stars would not be quenched. Then the sky spirits swept the seven sisters into the heavens where they became a new constellation. To this day, the Pleiades remind us that men and women, although different, are equally strong.

SEVEN SISTERS

The Message of Seven Sisters

We often joke about differences between the genders to diffuse a very real tension. Men evolved to understand the world physically: to set aside emotions until they have the luxury of processing them, to spend long hours tracking in silence, to pursue and defend. Women evolved to understand the world intuitively: to communicate during group activities, to notice nonverbal signals from the youngest in their care, to select ripe berries based on years of ingrained experience. No wonder there's trouble!

In ancient times, the elder council eased the tension. Senior men discussed how events might affect the prosperity of the clan and other tribes. Senior women considered the emotional and psychological needs of individuals and the group. Every aspect of the community's physical and spiritual health was balanced against the others.

The seven sisters are extraordinary because they balanced different kinds of knowledge within themselves. They understood both masculine and feminine, physical and spiritual. When they added the pains of men to their pains as women, their wisdom surpassed that of the elders before their bodies had ripened enough to marry.

Taking on both male and female knowledge is dangerous. It requires one body and mind to bear the suffering of two genders. Yet sometimes that's exactly what women do...they carry their own burdens while shouldering those of a man. Single mothers protect and nurture their children while unmarried women build lives alone. Husbands grow ill or stumble so wives carry them for a month, a year, a lifetime. Widows become their own mates.

Today we are integrating the knowledge of the elder council, of both genders, into every level of society. Our schools and universities burst with female teachers and professors. Our businesses recognize the unique benefits of feminine leadership. Our highest courts understand that women from all backgrounds are wise, that their histories and experiences are critical to true justice.

Valuing women's perspectives has an additional benefit: it allows us to more fully value the contributions of men. In tribal structures, a man's reputation was based on what he did for the community. The best hunter and the highest earner provide no value if they hoard what they have hunted. Today, men who cannot achieve within a narrowly defined role are looked down on while "successful" men gobble up more than their share. Our modern society therefore does not truly honor a man's strengths and abilities.

When a man's identity is linked with iron chains to wealth or power, everyone suffers. Nations that focus only on tangible assets like economic stability and military strength lack the intangible assets of compassion and empathy. There is no use for grain stored in such vast quantities that it rots; there is no value to money hoarded in such quantities that it exists only as a numeric concept. A balanced society will distribute excess grain to those in need. A balanced person will utilize excess funds to bolster community projects.

The negative cycle of gender imbalanced is linked in other ways, too. When women's contributions are devalued, the man who performs the ultimate acts of strength—being a single father, carrying a wife through illness, allowing compassion to enhance his leadership—walks a gauntlet of social ridicule. He is "weak," "soft," "pussy-whipped," "gay." Gender-based terms make him womanly and therefore ineffectual. His strength is neutered by a brawny line between the sexes. *Approach that line,* men are told, *and become less than you were.*

The most important message from the Pleiades is that our natural state is one of mutual strength. The oldest sister did not want to physically become a man or to fulfill only a man's role. Nor did she seek to place women above men. Disenfranchising the men would have been as destructive as disenfranchising the women. Any society that values either gender more than the other is a society divided.

Back in the early days of the Dreamtime, the sisters were honored for their unique accomplishment. Despite having earned that respect, they had to be removed from the ancient world. Their dual perspective would have made their lives unbearable. Other women would not have been able to understand their knowledge of men; men would not have been able to relate to them as they did to other women. Their unique viewpoint would have caused the sisters an excessive amount of suffering.

Modern society has the opportunity to do what the sisters could not. During the last century, women and men have taken on each other's knowledge. Single parents, people who delay marriage or choose not to marry, widows and widowers have learned how to be protector and nurturer, provider and comforter. Now we can welcome people who hold this dual perspective. We can let their strength shine like stars burning among us.

This is the sacred message both genders have known since people first gathered into groups...that either gender can bear the burden for both. That the hearts of men and women are big enough and their arms are strong enough to carry a spouse, a family, a friend. This deeply spiritual love disappears only when we agree to hide it away. We are weak only when we choose to believe the modern myths that spring from issues of power and control, insecurity and instability.

These issues affect every nation in our modern world. In the U.S., much is made of the fact that religious restrictions in some countries bar women from receiving an education. Yet American fundamentalists from several popular religions bar women from becoming spiritual leaders or heads of household. Unwed mothers are maligned while absentee fathers, who conveniently bear no overt signs of their "sins," are spared any repercussions.

Our secular society is still influenced by these judgments. Education means little if it can never be used; employment is psychologically degrading when the wage gap between genders exceeds twenty percent; a woman making a bid for president is merely a footnote when few corporations have any female executives.

Yet the issue is not solely based in gender dynamics. Not when a college degree costs six figures, not when blue-collar workers are indentured by low wages and lower status. Domestic violence—against husbands and wives, children and elders—is driven in part by an economic model that pays too little for many people to support their families. The poorest among us are disenfranchised by a system that doesn't respect the contributions of every person.

Our societies have changed from tribes to nations, from neighborhoods to a global community. We are each responsible for improving our own society so it can improve the world. We are also responsible for sharing what we can with our far-flung neighbors. Our foreign sisters do not deserve fewer rights simply because they were born into systems mired in issues of power and control; our worldwide brothers also deserve to have their contributions fully valued.

In times of darkness, we need only look up to remember our power. The Pleiades, burning brightly for millennium, honor the sisterhood of mankind and the brotherhood of humanity. The way requires suffering, some of it harsh, and we will sometimes have to bear each others' burdens. Together we can celebrate equality and strength. Together we can lift free of our individual bodies. Together we can shine.

War

Long ago, animals and birds mingled easily. Cormorants settled in the swampy northern region with kangaroos. Death adders felt at home with possums in the rainforest while cockatoos hung out with koalas in eucalyptus groves. Territories meant little and boundaries didn't exist.

Because the swamps had few pockets of dry land, water birds built nests on mounds of marsh grass. But the animals couldn't tell the difference between the grass and a bird's home, so they couldn't always avoid the nests. Every year a few eggs were accidentally cracked or broken. The chicks never knew when a clumsy paw would upend their lives.

After a while, the birds banned the animals from the lakes and rivers. Low-lying areas that flooded during the wet season were also off limits. The animals followed the new rules to keep the peace. For the rest of the year, they avoided the swamps and marshes. Nestlings thrived.

But the birds had kept all the best watering spots for themselves. When the dry season set in, the animals realized they had been given creeks and billabongs that held water only during the wet season. Ponds disappeared. Rivers flowed only with mud.

Whenever desperate creatures headed north to the permanent water sources, birds pecked and clawed and screamed until they turned back. By the time the monsoon rains fell months later, all the animals would be dead. Their only choice was to take the water by force. They had to declare war.

They mustered every wallaby and kangaroo, every crocodile and goanna, every rat and mouse and spiny echidna and snake. As they moved north, the sound they made was like a terrible avalanche. Claws pierced the ground and tails lashed the dust. Fur bristled and muzzles twitched. Dingoes drooled at the thought of slaking their thirst with blood.

At the southernmost point of the wetlands, the birds gathered their own forces. Cranes and herons stood as thick as river reeds. Flocks of galahs thousands strong wheeled overhead. Cockatoos crowded the trees and flipped their yellow crests like angry blooms. They would not to yield a single puddle or an inch of ground.

The battle began. The screams and the struggles and the hate threw up a sheen of red...red dust, red sound, red blood. Bodies piled up. Blood caked the dust and spattered the leaves; it stained the rocks and gloomed the waters.

Only two creatures stood aside. Owl had been asleep when the fighting had begun and so hadn't been recruited by the birds. Flying Fox, a bat that eats only fruit, couldn't bear to harm either side. She was half bird and half animal. Joining either group meant killing her brothers and sisters.

Owl was a crafty fellow. He said that if they didn't fight, they would be considered traitors. And since Flying Fox was related to both sides, she couldn't risk joining whichever side would eventually lose. The survivors would hate her because she would remind them of the conquering enemy.

In this war, her only true ally was Owl. She had to follow his advice. The pair joined the side that appeared to be winning. As soon as the advantage shifted, they turned and fought for the other group. They switched loyalties as quickly as the wind, making allies of strangers and strangers of friends.

There seemed no end to the war. After days and weeks of carnage, the sun could no longer bear to watch. It fled so far into the heavens darkness fell at midday. The battle finally stopped. For the first time, both sides realized how thickly the bodies lay.

SEVEN SISTERS

They vowed to settle their differences after they brought back the light.

Owl could see well enough in the dark to fly, so the others asked him to coax the sun back to its usual place. He laughed. This was much better than being on the winning side. In a world of darkness, he was king. The groups that had been fighting for dominance were suddenly ruled by a single heartless creature.

While Owl screeched about his newfound power, Flying Fox slipped from her roost. She flew toward that far-away place where the light had hidden itself away. No bird or animal had ever dared to travel that far before. Only the wind had come close, and even it could accompany her only part of the way. When Fox had flown past the last breeze and could no longer hear the whisper of her own wings, she knew she was truly alone.

Her shoulders burned with every flap. Despite the agony, she kept flying until the stars blinked out of sight. Finally she saw a speck of light. It was no bigger than a mulga seed yet it burned fiercely. It was Sun, as yet still a galaxy away.

As she closed the distance, the light turned toward her. Its magnificent intensity nearly made her swoon. She forgot her pain and drifted in gentle updrafts. As the pair returned across the galaxy, Fox felt only a continuous euphoria.

When the leading rays of light touched the earth, they fired the strangest and most beautiful dawn ever. The creatures celebrated by assigning every species to a suitable home. Death adders slithered into the central desert while blue-tongued lizards kept to the limestone plateau. Piebald geese were satisfied with Kakadu's marshlands and scrub turkeys darted into the jungles.

Today the birds and animals still live in the places they were assigned long ago. Whenever Flying Fox emerges at dusk, the creatures leave her in peace. If Owl dares to show his face before dark, though, he is mobbed by flocks of angry birds.

LAINE CUNNINGHAM

The Message of War

Animals and birds are connected by the energy of creation, by the Dreaming. When rats store up food, some of the seeds sprout into plants that feed many animals. In times of famine, Aboriginal people knew that ants gathered enough tiny acacia seeds to make a meal. The sheer diversity of life helps everything survive.

Our various societies are as important to the web of life as different species. Cultures differ in part because each evolved in a certain landscape. Geography has as much to do with who we are as any philosophy. A society's mores, then, can be as critical to our planet as good stewardship. In celebrating divisions of geography and lifestyle, culture and belief, we should always remember that we are all related.

Unfortunately, humans enjoy taking sides. At times, carrying a banner is necessary. Many causes are righteous, fulfilling concepts of justice brings us peace, and sometimes force is needed to prevent genocide or oppression. War, too, is occasionally the only option. Even Buddha condoned the execution of one man when it would spare the lives of hundreds.

Our unique brains with their talent for arguments and words, posturing and pontificating should never eclipse our common humanity. If we stay calm during adversity, we discover opportunity. We can fight over resources or share with those who are less fortunate. We can turn a blind eye to human rights violations or insist that governments rule with compassion. We can feel self-righteous about our freedoms or we can support our foreign brothers and sisters as they battle oppression.

The adjustment required to achieve the new perspective feels as broad as a galaxy but really is only the width of an atom. When we temper our view with compassion, the same mechanisms that encourage us to take sides can eliminate sides.

SEVEN SISTERS

The need for war falls away. We recognize that different isn't better or worse. Even cultural mores that seem strange are necessary to the web of life.

Before we can merge this perspective into our thought process, we must recognize the difference between duality and polarity. Duality sets opposing forces against each other and assumes that conflict is inevitable. Polarity balances necessary opposites. If the birds had recognized that both sides deserved the best they could have achieved together, war would not have been necessary.

This message is especially important to our global society. What seems contained to one group or region always has worldwide repercussions. The oceans and mountain ranges that used to buffer people and their beliefs now are crossed electronically at the speed of thought. Our technology has upgraded our planetary social network; now we must upgrade our minds.

The wars of today prove this need. They are increasingly over resources...oil, territories, and even the resources of the human heart. Because they are mired in duality, militants exterminate themselves through their insistence on violence. Leaders reject the measured, compassionate approach as weak. They forget that their own people will suffer.

Negotiation and compromise turn duality into polarity. Diplomacy is as much a part of the war machine as blood and bombs; it is the brake that can stop the tanks from rolling. Mobilizing for war is itself a negotiation because the standoff allows opposing parties to size up each other's forces, motivation and intent. Even the first wave of troops offers another opportunity to compromise.

The tactics don't always end in a truce. Every step can go astray. The birds began with a righteous cause but tangled their negotiations with trickery. They thought that by owning all the permanent water sites they would hold all the power. Arrogance led to a drastic miscalculation when they refused to negotiate. No matter how poor the animals' chances, war was the only path that offered any hope of survival.

When others ask for help, they shouldn't be seen as weak. The request might be the start of a negotiation for their fair share of some resource. The longstanding struggle between Israel and Palestine is less about land than mutual respect; in America, the cries of the poor are less about money than the right of all people to earn a living wage. How we respond to the request tells us how we feel about our own stability. Only tyrants fear fairness.

Polarity also tells us why life entails so much suffering. The birds tried to create an ideal world where accidents never harmed their chicks and nests were never disturbed. Their utopian model could arise only if they denied other creatures what was rightfully theirs. Polarity exists only when everyone's needs are considered. Often that means everyone shares the suffering.

Things will never be entirely fair, and pain and joy will never be distributed equally. But human consciousness can temper the imbalance. This challenge is one of the reasons our souls incarnate in this world; human nature is hardwired to seek the light. A true Utopia is a world in which we support each other. Perhaps that is the real purpose of suffering: it creates the ability to recognize other people's pain, and it drives us to ease that pain any way we can.

The ancient tales warn that we will never achieve lasting peace. Man has fought his shadow side for thousands of years and will struggle against it for thousands to come. True to the rule of polarity, this internal darkness creates one of our brightest glories. When we seek the ideal, when we negotiate and compromise with compassion and love, we have already created our paradise.

Here we fully recognize the message of the sun. Its light shines on everyone equally; it mirrors the light that radiates from our hearts. When we stick to ideals founded in our own life's details or when we feel need so deeply that we harm other tribes, nations or beliefs, we lose our light and warmth. To find the true path, we must temper our logic with love.

There is a difference between knowing something logically and holding a belief in our hearts. The type of understanding that comes from the mind tells us to store up far more than we can ever use against future calamity. It divides the world into categories for and against, and tries to eliminate duality by exterminating that which is different than itself.

The understanding of the heart is far different. It assures us that diversity is an asset. Polarity supports the cultural and social web that is as critical to our survival as biological diversity. When we recognize that both suffering and joy are part of the human condition, the heart eliminates duality by releasing fear.

Sometimes finding our light takes as much effort as a fruit bat needs to fly across the galaxy. When we finally draw near to our heart's glow, we are buoyed by divine updrafts. We discover that each of us is a sun on this earth. No division separates a bird from an animal or a human from a tree. We truly are connected in the web of life, in this continuous Dreamtime.

When we accept our place in the Dreaming, we recognize that searching for Utopia is wasteful. It demands a singular, exclusive version of perfection in a universe that embraces polarity; it tries to eliminate suffering when to do so would also eliminate compassion. The shadows of night fall on us all. Even if our light is only the size of a tiny mulga seed, the intensity of its glow can illuminate the world.

The Prank

According to traditional law, a man who was strong and capable might take more than one wife. Of course, he had to earn the respect of the women first. Since women met most of their family's needs, including providing meat by hunting small game, multiple wives meant more hands could share the load. As long as the man was loving and contributed his share of the labor, the arrangement worked for everyone.

One young man worked very hard to impress the women he wanted to marry. Other men looked for beauty or grace or thighs that could carry the weight of many children. This man considered only the women's backs, the muscles of their arms, and how much bush tucker they gathered in bowls called coolamons.

Back then, no one could marry until they had matured. Love and physical pleasure were intense experiences that couldn't be rushed into. It was particularly important that men didn't launch into sexual activity before they understood its special circumstances. If they did, they were more likely to end up without the proper respect for women.

The young man who liked the strong women meticulously observed the social taboos between the genders. After his initiation he'd never again spoken directly to his sisters, as was proper. He never spoke to the young women he liked and instead interacted only with their mothers. Soon he had the respect of the elders, the mothers, and the strong daughters. When the time was right, he took his first wife. He provided well for her and they started a family. After a few years, he had married every one of the strong women.

Then a prolonged drought set in. Everyone worked hard just to survive. But the man with many wives stopped hunting as often. Soon he grew lax in his camp duties, so lax that the elder council berated him repeatedly. He had what he wanted, though. Why should he work, especially when there was no chance to achieve his former glory?

Eventually the rains returned, as they always do, and the land was fertile again. But laziness had replaced the man's good habits. After the midday meal, he wandered off to snooze in the shade. He always napped under a certain waratah tree far from any camp noise. It was amazing, really, that he could sleep as much as he did but his appetite for rest was surpassed only by his appetite for food. He grew fat from the labor of his wives.

No one was happy with the situation, least of all the wives. As he trundled off for his nap one day, the women glanced at each other over their grinding stones. They waited a short time then crept to the waratah tree where he snored with his flabby cheeks jiggling. Moving carefully, they carried him to a hollow log and stuffed him inside.

He woke with a start but it was too late. The log was dark and dusty, and he couldn't take a breath without coughing. The many hands of his wives, made even stronger by their labor, held his kicking legs as they wedged his round belly inside. They sealed up the ends with mud that the sun baked into hard plugs.

Days passed. The husband wriggled and squirmed, hot and hungry but unable to move an inch. His arms were positioned over his head. When his thirst became unbearable, he bit them and lapped up the blood. Eventually he lost weight and was able to inch down and kick free.

Although he was weak, anger made the world swim in a blurry cloud. He cut long branches from the strongest mulga shrubs and sharpened the tips. After hardening the stakes in a fire, he waded into his wives' favorite billabong. He set so many stakes in the mud even a snake couldn't slip between them. The murky water hid the deadly trap, and the husband hid in the bushes.

Soon enough his wives came to the billabong. The youngest two ran ahead and threw themselves into the cool depths. Their eyes had not seen the stakes but their bodies found them well enough. Blood stained the water like strange ochre.

The husband laughed and shouted and cried. As he ran off into the bush, every patch of red earth rippled like the bloody billabong. He could not understand his actions; he could only think that his wives had cast a spell on him before they'd stuffed him into that hollow log. Why had he responded to a prank with such a terrible crime?

He'd never thought he could slaughter women yet his arms had been singed by the fire that had hardened the stakes. His thighs still bled from when he had tested the sharp points on himself. The superficial wounds bore witness to the deadly wounds he had given his wives. He'd murdered, he'd murdered women, and he'd acted in a way that was unbefitting a man.

The dead women's brothers and fathers tracked him down. The loose skin on the husband's arms and thighs snagged on thorns and left a clear blood trail. Even when the posse trapped him in a deep wash, the husband still hoped to avoid justice. He hopped around trying to dodge the deadly spears. The skin on his arms flapped like ridiculous wings.

As the spears found his belly and legs and neck, his arms continued moving. When his body finally toppled, his spirit flew away with some of his bones and flesh. The loose, floppy skin tightened and became wings. The lies he shrieked about his wives pitched so high people could no longer hear them. To this day, the bat is still called the spirit of death.

SEVEN SISTERS

The Message of The Prank

Aboriginal tribes often used hollow logs as coffins. When the wives locked their lazy husband inside a coffin, they were saying he was as much good to them as a corpse. Since his imprisonment forced him to go without food, he experienced the same deprivation he caused his tribe by refusing to hunt. Just as the strength of a log is lost to decay, the value of the husband was lost to laziness.

The message in this tale strikingly addresses greed, power and control in domestic relationships. Marital roles were an important issue in ancient cultures, and they continue to be important today. Love, honor and respect are not just pretty words. When the husband refused to honor his duties or respect his wives' efforts, his love seemed to have been reserved only for the warmth in his belly.

Marriage has always been a kind of contract. Each partner had responsibilities that often were assigned by gender. Today gender roles are far less important. Husbands might stay home with the kids and wives are frequently the primary earner. As couples negotiate household chores and budgets, love enables them to work around individual needs and desires. Honor and respect create a strong foundation for their efforts.

Without honor, neither person will bring their best to the relationship. Without respect, daily negotiations degenerate into insults, silence, or a formal politeness that glosses over the issues. Without love, of course, there is no reason to stay together...not for economic stability, not for convenience or social status or to preserve a certain image...not at all. Not even children, the excuse repeated like a mantra across America, should trap a couple in anything less than love.

This isn't to say people should abandon ship the moment things sour. The deep and biding affection that leads to marriage often guides the way through challenges. But once counseling is over or has been rejected, once physical and emotional intimacy have decayed and the house is as hollow as a log, it's time to split. Both individuals will be free to seek out new relationships that serve their hearts.

This is true even if children are in the picture. It's always a mistake to stay together solely for their benefit. The parents could be shining examples of perfect mothers and fathers but a foundered marriage will negatively affect the family. Children might not be old enough to express what they feel and older children might be too insecure to speak their minds. Yet they understand far more than most adults want to admit.

When I was young, my parents became lifelong friends with another couple. My father's military career kept our family on the move, so knowing the same people for many years stands out in my mind. The other couple separated for a while. The husband stayed with us but his attempt to kick alcohol didn't go well. My brother and I found bottles stashed in the strangest places.

In an effort to give their children a stable environment, the wife took him back. As long as he kept his addiction under control, she thought the kids would never know. When her eldest was eleven, he sat her down for a talk. He and his sister had wondered for years when she was going to get a divorce. For the family's sake, they asked her to cut him loose. Sometimes kids know what needs to happen better than grownups.

Addiction is an extreme example but damage can also be done by "less critical" issues. When parents stick with loveless relationships, they teach their children a miserable lesson. Kids might learn that women should indenture themselves to a spouse or the family, or that men should suppress their true selves inside the home. Fighting in secret prevents the children from learning mature ways to resolve conflict. Even the hard work of building a new life after divorce is rich with opportunities.

Bad marriages also change the couple's relationships with others. In the story, the lazy man lost more than just the respect of his wives. Other men no longer considered him reliable and the esteem of the elders gave way to contempt. He was like the heroes—of sports, of industry, of the stock market, whatever—who trip over obstacles they thought the public would never discover. Their glory shines only in their own memories.

The damage done by sham marriages doesn't stop there. When one partner doesn't pull his or her weight because the relationship is all but over, the overworked partner functions less and less efficiently. That person no longer has the energy to support coworkers, friends and neighbors, or members of the extended family. As the marriage becomes ever more Sisyphean, larger ripples disturb a broader swath of the community.

What costs the local community also costs the larger society. Clinging to a bad marriage shrinks the pool of potential partners for singles who are ready for healthy relationships. Affairs arranged out of spite or a desperate need for affection siphon off time and effort that otherwise would support positive activities. The animosity that builds when divorce is delayed prevents couples from being fully productive.

No matter how hard the parents try to protect the children, kids raised by loveless couples learn that marriage is distasteful. By conscious choice or unconscious arrangement, some boys and girls will reject any long-term commitment. More often they will replicate the broken relationship model they were taught. The impact of a dysfunctional marriage therefore resonates across generations.

In Aboriginal society, the love, honor and respect husbands and wives held for each other had parallels outside of marriage. Each person was born into a specific category that governed how individuals were related. The categories, called moieties, eliminated inbreeding and ensured respect for all people, whether related by blood or law. Love affairs that crossed moiety boundaries, failure to respect others, and murder were all "wrong-way" acts that were contrary to the Dreaming law.

Any wrong-way act disrupted the flow of energy and threatened the clans, their land, and the survival of the entire world. Spearing the lazy husband returned the suffering he caused the wives, soothed the anger of the victims' relatives, demonstrated the consequences of crime, and rebalanced the world's energy. The posse acted not only for their sisters but for all humanity and planet Earth.

The law doesn't change just because a couple thinks they can hide the wrong-way events taking place inside their marriage. Life partners must respect each other whether or not they seek (or are able to seek) the legal bond of marriage. Even outside of romantic ties, society must encourage respect and universal love. By following that path, we create a right-way world. Then all our relationships will be strong.

The Orphan

Long ago, a man wandered the desert. He was an odd fellow with thick legs and stumpy arms. His eyes were close together and his heavy lids made him look as if he was half asleep. This man had always been alone, or so he thought; he couldn't remember a time when he'd had a family or a tribe to call his own. He was truly an orphan.

Whenever the orphan came across a clan or even a small family, he followed like a dingo in their wake. While the dogs looked for scraps of food, the man sought whatever scrap of kindness someone might toss him. But groups small and large drove him away. They had no desire to take on so odd a stranger, especially one without many skills.

Finally the orphan settled near the only clan that tolerated his presence. So long as he stayed outside the camp and didn't bother the women, they let him live in peace. He found solace in the sounds of children playing and men talking. If he closed his eyes, he could pretend he was part of the group. What lovely daydreams those were.

A river ran near where the clan lived. Every morning women filled oblong bowls called coolamons with water. They carried the bowls back to camp and tucked them under thick shrubs to keep the water cool. When certain plants were in bloom, flowers were added to the water to create a fragrant, sweet drink.

Whenever the orphan asked for a sip of water, the people waved him away or chased him up a tree. It didn't matter if the water was nectar-sweetened or plain, freshly drawn or hot from having sat in the sun; their reaction was always the same.

I have to provide for myself, the orphan thought, *while they have plenty of hands to share the work.*

The more he thought about the unfairness of it, the more he gnawed at the leaves of the tree in which he lived. The fibers were tough and eucalyptus oil stung his lips but he didn't notice. He was too bound up in his frustration and too busy plotting his revenge.

One day all the men went hunting and the women and children left to gather bush tucker. When everyone was out of sight, the orphan crept into the empty camp. Coolamons were everywhere. Many held mulga seeds that would be roasted then ground into a paste. Others were stacked with skewers of dried *Solanums,* a small fruit that tasted like melon. Bush plums, bush raisins and emu fat had been stored in others.

The orphan grabbed all the coolamons. He scattered the seeds the women had so carefully cleaned. He broke the skewers and trampled the dried *Solanums.* Grubs were crushed under his feet and bush potatoes broke open in the dust. Days of labor was destroyed in minutes.

The orphan dragged the empty bowls down to the river. Working as quickly as his stumpy arms allowed, he filled the coolamons with water. He then balanced each bowl on the limbs of a sturdy shrub. The sun was blistering hot but he never stopped. By the time he filled the last coolamon, the river had become a channel of sticky mud.

He climbed into the shrub and painted special symbols on the branches. Chanting powerful words, he forced the shrub to grow as high as the towering gum trees. He kept chanting until the shrub was twice as tall then twice again. Only the eagle ever flew that high. The people would never reach the water they thought too dear to share.

Let them weep, he thought as he gnashed at the leaves. *Let them drink their own tears!*

SEVEN SISTERS

The women returned to camp first. When they saw the food scattered about, the sounds of a great confusion rose to the orphan's perch. The men ran back and began preparing for war. Surely their enemies had destroyed their stores. Surely their enemies should pay!

A young woman found a single empty coolamon under a pile of spinifex grass and headed to the river to get water for the elders. When she saw that the river had disappeared, she couldn't help but scream. Terror swept through the clan. The same disaster that had dried up the water might also dry up their lives.

The orphan felt a terrible, piercing glee. The longer the panic continued, the harder it was to suppress his giggles and snorts. He stuffed leaves in his mouth to muffle the sound. Although the people didn't hear him, one woman noticed the unusual tree. When the men found the stones the orphan had used to grind the paint, they knew magic was the cause of their troubles.

They spotted the orphan high up in the branches. Two brothers known for their strength and courage immediately scaled the trunk. The orphan wasn't worried. He had made the tree far too tall for anyone to climb. No matter how much the men tried, they would never reach him. An orphan with stumpy limbs and few skills had conquered them all.

But the brothers were as relentless as dingoes following a blood trail. Even as the trunk grew thin and branches clawed at their eyes, they always knew where to put their feet. The orphan edged up higher. Still the brothers came, gripping the powdery bark with hands that never slipped.

I made the tree tall enough, the orphan thought. *I made it tall enough!*

He was wrong. The brothers pried him from the trunk and threw him to the ground. The entire tribe closed around him. Men used *waddies,* clubs made from hardwood, to beat him mercilessly. The women were so outraged they broke their digging sticks against his stumpy form.

Somehow he escaped without any broken bones. He grew fur to protect himself from the sun and stayed high up in the tallest gum trees from then on. Never again would he touch a drop of water. Instead he ate gum leaves to slake his thirst. Whenever koala's descendants are hunted for food, their bones are never broken to honor the orphan's ability to survive the harsh punishment.

The Message of The Orphan

Do you have a friend you can only tolerate for a few hours? Maybe that person complains too much or is a touch too chatty. You love them but after a while, you need a break from their personality. Imagine being in a hunter-gatherer clan with that person. Every day you would have to interact with him or her, probably more than you would like.

Many cultures that lived in small bands dealt with lazy, needy and irritating people by shuffling them off to other clans. Whenever the burden got too great, people would remind Aunt Chatty or Uncle Annoying about someone they hadn't seen in a while…someone who was part of a different group. Aunt Chatty would take the hint and go live with the other clan for a time.

If Uncle Annoying was too annoying to take the hint, he would be ordered to go with the other group because they had better resources. They might actually have had fewer resources but everyone pretended they didn't to save face for Uncle A. Clans were linked by blood and social ties as strong as blood, so the other band was obligated to shoulder its share of the human burden.

Perhaps something like that had happened to the man who became a koala. Perhaps he had experienced something worse. He wasn't a child, yet he was considered an orphan. He had no

SEVEN SISTERS

ties to any tribe...he claimed no brothers or fathers, no uncles or grandfathers. Since Aboriginal society made a relative of nearly everyone within and between clans, his barren status was unusual.

Ultimately the fact that he was an orphan doesn't seem to serve any purpose in the story...not overtly, anyway. Aboriginal people would have understood a clear message, though. Even today when tribal members meet, they tell each other their lineage. By trading family names, they discover how they are related. Then they know how to treat each other...as sisters or cousins, for example.

It sounds convoluted to people whose society emphasizes only the nuclear family but in tribal traditions, all relationships are important. Understanding how you are connected tells you how to behave around other people. It also provides you with a way to get whatever help you might need. To have no ties in that type of society is to be truly bereft.

The clan in this story was under no obligation to offer the orphan any assistance. Since they weren't related even by the weakest social thread, merely tolerating his presence could be taken for kindness. Yet other visitors would have become cousins or nieces or uncles over time. When the orphan's treatment is compared to the usual reception offered to strangers, it's clear that tolerance is far removed from true compassion.

The orphan was so far outside the social structure that he could be completely ignored. By the time he sought revenge, physical need had nothing to do with his anger. He drank alone at the river. He foraged alone, and even when he slept in trees near the camp he was alone. In all those lonely days no one offered him the smallest kindness, not even a drink of water.

We often talk these days about the breakdown of social structures. Email and texting have replaced personal communication, and television is a poor substitute for human interaction. Our elderly live on islands of nursing care communities, single parents operate without the support of other adults, and immigrants arrive in our country without friends or family. Multiple factors contribute to these issues but one cause rises above them all: our skewed perspective on love.

Ironically, love between two people has evolved into an exclusive and exclusionary club. The rights and advances and social changes that were supposed to free our hearts have trapped people in a constricting bond. Marriage itself is a fine thing. But any relationship that cuts ties to the rest of the world or that limits our relationships with others is no better than an arranged union.

Through this strange evolution, our modern clan has shrunk to a single person: a spouse or lover. Oh, we chat with clients and coworkers, and we even wave pleasantly at our neighbors. But if you are divorced or separated or single or widowed, you are an orphan. Even people who are married or romantically involved can practically be orphans because couples often neglect their other relationships.

Our culture also puts couples on a pedestal. Romantic relationships have been raised so far beyond their true value that couples have been excised from the social network. What used to be one part of a full life has become a pass-fail system. People judge themselves and each other based on whether they are married, how many times they have divorced, and even whether they lost a partner to illness or accident. "Never married" equals undesirable, "divorced" makes for damaged goods, and "widowed" means forever in mourning. We are more than these labels...and more than the sum of our romance.

The most insidious result of this inflated value lies within the relationships. Couples often cut themselves off from old friends...especially single friends. The isolation makes it impossible for the couple to serve anyone except themselves or, occasionally, other couples. It also creates an unhealthy alliance in which each partner must magically meet a hundred percent of the other's needs.

No one person can fulfill so great a role. Meaningful human connections are as varied as food gathered from the bush. Buddies are different than friends, and coworkers are different than peers. We can no more rely solely on a romantic partner than we can reject water and live only on food. Only Koala has succeeded in that, and his choice dooms him to gnawing on tough, bitter leaves.

Our social network is the pool into which we dive after a stressful day; our personal connections have their own rhythms and tides. The network doesn't always trigger a rush of new thoughts and ideas, although it might. We do not always touch the depths that support us during crisis, although it's possible. None of it can exist if we separate couples from their clans and make them into orphans.

Realistically, of course, not every stray can be treated like family and bit players cannot be allowed to consume more resources than they return. But the orphan didn't demand meat or bush tucker. He didn't warm himself by the clan's fires or crash their celebrations. A sip of water now and then would not have created hardship. A sip of water now and then would have softened his isolation. The kindness of the offer would have made him happy.

By restricting our interactions only to a spouse or significant other, we are as stingy as the clan that ignored a lonely orphan. We should never think or act as if love is a limited resource. Compassion, empathy and kindness are all expressions of love. Simple gestures and the relationships they support are as valuable as the bonds formed through romantic love.

The human heart has no limitations. And in a society that tends to isolate its members, a small act of kindness can be like a river in the desert.

Hunger

Mothers always took their children along to gather bush foods like native cherries and mulga seeds. Women also hunted small game like snakes and lizards. Their daily efforts provided nearly all the food their families needed. When men killed a kangaroo or an emu, the meat was distributed to the entire camp. That way widows, elders and the ill received enough protein.

Whatever meat a woman received from the hunters was hers to divide among her children. Even if a child's father or uncles or brother had made a kill, boys got all their meat from their mothers. Not until the boys became adults would they begin to provide for others. The initiation ceremony usually took place between eight and twelve years of age, so the boys had plenty of time to learn about bush foods from their mothers.

One boy had seen many of his friends taken to their initiations. The ceremony took weeks and was performed in a secret place away from camp. When the initiates returned, they performed adult duties and took no interest in childish games. The boys had died. Men had been born in their place.

The young boy suspected that his own initiation was near. But he loved his mother with the fierceness of a bushfire and couldn't bear to be separated from her. When his uncles came for him, he clung to her waist. Wrapped in her strong arms, he thought that his uncles would not win, that he and his mother would be together forever. Then the men dragged him into the bush.

When they arrived at the bora ground, the place where the ceremony would be performed, it was worse than the boy had feared. Strange symbols had been drawn on the ground with seeds and stones. The ground paintings were rimmed with plant fluff that shivered in the breeze as if it held the Dreaming power. Perhaps that was how initiates died: they were eaten by the symbol and spat out later as something else.

That wouldn't happen to him. Let the men have their strange songs and secret ceremonies. Let the boys who were dumb enough to stay be gobbled up! The moment his uncles let go, he took off running. He shook the men who gave chase and followed the river home.

Back at camp, the elders looked at him with long faces. They were disappointed, of course, but the boy had no thoughts for them. When he found his mother, they held each other and wept with joy. Then he asked her for meat. She roasted a goanna, a monitor lizard, until the crisp skin leaked clear, fragrant juice. The boy ate every last scrap.

Late that evening a few of the uncles returned. They looked everywhere but the boy had hidden in a cave atop a nearby plateau. The men wouldn't go there because the spirits of the dead lived underground. The spirits frightened the boy, too, but at least they wouldn't keep him from his mother.

Eventually his uncles returned to the bora ground. Other initiates were waiting so the men couldn't waste all their time on one child. The boy emerged only when his mother climbed the plateau the next morning. She offered him wild oranges and seedcakes but he ate only meat. When he asked for more, she fetched the dried meat she'd stored up. Only after the boy had eaten every chunk did he finally feel satisfied.

Day after day, morning and evening the boy stayed hidden in the cave. Whatever the mother had gathered—witchetty grubs, succulent lizards and bustard eggs—disappeared into her son's mouth. Whenever a hunter gave her a cut of kangaroo or wallaby, she took that up to the plateau. The rest of the family made do with seedcakes and bush potatoes. Still the boy was hungry; still he demanded meat.

After a while, the initiates returned. The boy sat alone on the plateau watching the new men being welcomed into the tribe. Early the next morning the entire camp packed up their tools and weapons. Most of the bush tucker had been harvested from that area and needed to regenerate. The people would settle near a different water source in an area with plenty of food.

Even as the tribe began the long walk, the boy wouldn't come down. He feared the punishment he might face for having left the bora ground. So long as he stayed in the cave, he never had to face the consequences of his choice. He watched silently as everything he'd ever known moved away. His mother ran up the hill to hug him one last time.

Meat! he said. *Give me meat!*

She gave him the few bits she'd set aside during the feast for the new men. Then she followed the rest of her people across the arid plain. Although she straggled far behind, eventually the pair lost sight of each other.

Meat! the boy called. His voice echoed in the cave behind him.

He sat down to wait. Near dusk his mother returned with the carcass of a bird. He devoured the kill and demanded more. But she had already started the long walk back and did not hear his cries.

For a short time she brought him whatever meat she could. The journey didn't leave much time to look for food so the boy's hunger was never satisfied. But the meat came from his mother's hand. It fed his fierce love.

One morning the boy waited for a long time. The sun churned through the sky, the stars lit one by one and the moon climbed its arcing path; still she did not come. The boy's stomach shrank and growled. Perhaps the camp had moved again and the walk was too long. Perhaps she had been given so much meat she couldn't carry it all. Whatever the reason, he would have to go to her.

He set off. He wasn't sure exactly where the new camp was but with a little luck, he would find his mother while she was out hunting. Finally he saw her. She was hunched over as if burdened by a great weight...an entire wallaby, perhaps, or at least the haunch of a kangaroo.

As he drew closer, his feet slowed. She hadn't moved since he'd spotted her. She wasn't digging nor did she seem to be looking for small game. Not until he stood in front of her did he realize the horror of her stillness.

She was dead. The *karadji*, the tribe's executioner, had speared both her thighs. The lances had pierced straight through her limbs before burying their points deep in the ground. Her body was propped up by the shafts in a grotesque parody of life. Her blood had turned the dust into lumpy seedcakes. The bloated carcass of a goanna, the boy's favorite kind of meat, lay beside her.

The sweet rot of her body made a thick stew of the air. With that meaty taste in his mouth, he ran all the way back to the plateau. He dove deep into the cave and hid where even the light couldn't penetrate. Hours passed or maybe days; he couldn't be sure. He knew only that he was too frightened to venture outside.

Eventually, of course, he had to. When he approached the mouth of the cave, the sunlight was as sharp as a spear point. He shuffled to the edge of the plateau, unsure how to quell his terrible hunger. As he stood there, an eagle struck him hard from behind.

A sharp pain flared in his mind. His neck had been broken and he tumbled off the plateau. The eagle, having meted out the boy's punishment, flew off to resume its own hunt for meat.

LAINE CUNNINGHAM

The Message of Hunger

The youth who refused to grow up was stuck in the child's self-centered world. He was emotionally stunted and didn't understand that others had needs. If he had been allowed to continue on that path, he would have consumed an increasing amount of resources while returning nothing to the tribe.

Anyone who has met a boy-man or a girl-woman knows the type: they resist working hard, they constantly blame others for their misfortune, they are quick to take and slow to give. Although their bodies have matured, they never accept adult responsibilities. Individuals who are capable yet unproductive devour a society's material resources. They also drain the emotional reserves of everyone around them.

In the story, the boy could not have remained a child without his mother's support. Although helping him meant providing less food and attention to the rest of her family, she stopped only when the executioner arrived. Today America is suffering from the same kind of dynamic: parents are shielding their children from the trials and pains that will make them into adults.

Studies conducted during the recent recession uncovered the problems associated with this trend. When given clearly defined rules and specific tasks, Gen Y employees performed well. When asked to utilize a little initiative, though, a surprising number were unable to function. Many of these individuals were also unable to accept guidance...they couldn't handle the feedback that would help them improve.

Although it seems strange, these traits weren't caused by a lack of structure or attention during their early years. Instead they were the result of overscheduled childhoods and fuzzy psychology. A week stuffed with tap dance, tuba lessons and softball leaves little time for a child to develop independently. It turns out that too much guidance is as harmful as too little.

Unfortunately, the trend is driven as often by ego as by concern for a child's potential. A son or daughter's schedule has become the modern parent's bling. The sacrifices made by adults score points in weekend brag fests. Today's helicopter parents are the Aboriginal mother who funneled scarce resources to her son while never pushing him to mature.

The issue is creating problems beyond the workplace. Since the ability to overschedule a child's life depends on wealth—that is, money to pay for the activities as well as the luxury of a parent's time—lower middle class and low-income families raise their children in a strikingly different manner. Today's parenting methods are therefore building a barrier between the workers, executives and leaders of tomorrow.

Our society will pay a heavy price. Entrepreneurs are far more valuable than corporations because they put money back into the economy while corporations put it into the pockets of wealthy CEOs. Yet our newest generation of workers is divided into segments that lack either entrepreneurial thinking or the financial stability and the higher education that opens doors. The next decade will bring new challenges because fewer adults will hold both sides of that equation.

Even the quality of interpersonal and community relations is being impacted by hyper-anxious parents. Children who have their every wish met make poor companions because they aren't used to compromise. Meanwhile, individuals raised in low-income and lower middle-class families lack the social network that can help them experience the broader world firsthand. Neither side understands the other's experiences, fears or goals. In a time when we take so much pride in freedom and civil rights, we are in danger of becoming a society divided by class.

Aboriginal mothers naturally resisted the death that awaited their sons yet they did not protect the boys from the trials that would help them mature. Perhaps modern parents have taken this detour because we have forgotten that the pain of the initiation rites is also born by the adults. Mothers mourned their sons' deaths so they could rejoice in the men who replaced them. The wounds the uncles inflicted on themselves during the final rite symbolized the sacrifices they had made to mold men out of boys.

Yet the adults did not, and today should not, take on all the suffering. The boys sacrificed bits of their bodies when circumcised, when a tooth was knocked out, or when blood was drawn. Girls sacrificed the blood and pain of their monthly flow. In return, they gained adult rights and responsibilities.

Somehow today's sons and daughters are expected to mature without having given up any of their youthful ease. A certain type of parent is too willing to make all the sacrifices on behalf of the children. Individuals raised this way believe that their status and wealth will only increase, that the ease of childhood will continue into their adult lives.

Here, too, we find the barrier between classes being strengthened. The sense of privilege imbued in the children of wealthier families is far different than the life lessons taught at a lower economic strata. For one set of young adults, their position is a right; for the other, it is a fight.

The deep irony is that children who have suffered—be it the loss of a parent to divorce or illness, sudden financial instability, multiple relocations, or even by giving up one goal to pursue another—are better equipped for life. This message isn't about values or goals or intellectual concepts that can change depending on cultural or ethnic backgrounds. Instead it's about a person's character, the fortitude and resilience that keeps them moving forward despite the odds.

Many of today's young adults understand compassion on an intellectual level but have never had to sacrifice their own needs for some larger gain. They know the rules yet have not written them on their hearts. How could they when they have been denied any opportunity to feel the depth of emotion required for true maturity? Even their joy is less profound because they are unable to compare it to their own suffering.

Because overly protective parenting has become a competition, children are also being cut off from lessons they might learn from other adults. Tribal cultures recognized that children need guidance from everyone in the community. In fact, fathers and mothers often were not involved in initiation ceremonies. Children learned that their lives were starting over, that their relationships with other adults would replace their reliance on their parents.

We can recreate this dynamic by involving our own tribes of aunts and uncles, friends and neighbors. Many people who are single or married, gay or straight, parents or childless can help our youth mature. The coach who builds discipline and self-confidence could be at school or right next door. The idol who sparks the drive to be a valued member of society might be a captain of industry or a stay-at-home spouse.

In connecting with adults who aren't their parents, kids learn about issues much different than those they've dealt with inside their family. This awakening to the larger world, the world they will soon navigate alone, prods them to put aside childish games and begin their own journeys. Some will take refuge in the cave of immaturity. As long as their parents make all the sacrifices, they will remain as spiritually muted as the dead souls that live underground.

In making men out of boys and women out of girls, we make our world a better place. The tribal structure has been replaced with an infinite pool of surrogates who represent many perspectives. This allows our social evolution to leap forward. By encouraging young adults to sacrifice the safety of childhood for the opportunities of maturity, we ensure that there will be plenty of meat for everyone.

 The Dance

Life in the far north of Australia was different than in the desert. There were kangaroos and cockatoos and gum trees, of course. There were also small crocodiles living in freshwater billabongs and large crocodiles that lurked in salt marshes. The estuaries breathed with the tide and termites built narrow mounds that always pointed north.

In this stunning place lived a stunning young woman. Her body was long and her limbs as supple as young cane. Adding to her beauty was a joy that poured out like the sudden monsoon rains. The touch of her hand was as soothing as the flush of cool river water through a mangrove swamp.

This woman loved to dance. She added new moves every day by mimicking different animals. When she saw a cormorant spread its wings to the sun, she threw her arms wide. The stomp of cockatoos along tree branches became part of her steps. And when the archer fish shot a perfect stream of water out of the marsh, she arched her back in that perfect curve.

Oh, how she loved to dance. She whirled and twirled for the sheer joy of movement, for the bliss of feeling the wind whisper across her skin. Men and women from every tribe stared. They couldn't help it; she was that radiant. Even the spirits that lived in the sky and the earth and the air watched her.

Despite the endless number of suitors who tried to woo her, she took neither a lover nor a husband. The chores of a wife and mother would leave little time for practice. A man might be known as a good hunter and a woman might spin hairstring that never frayed but everyone was expected to perform a variety of chores...even dancers who spun with their souls.

Although it wasn't unheard of for a woman to stay single, it was unusual. Many people didn't believe the dancer would remain dedicated to her art all her life. Her resistance, they assumed, was temporary. They couldn't imagine making that kind of sacrifice themselves so they were unable to imagine it in anyone else.

When those people talked about her and even when they talked to her, they claimed she would change. Her heart would long for a companion less fleeting than the wind. She would replace her passion with a husband and then a baby. Perhaps some of those people really did mean to help the dancer. Only they knew.

One man listened to the chatter with glee. This man could throw a spear farther than anyone else. He could spin a hunting boomerang so hard it would lodge in the trunk of a paperbark tree. His arms were knotted with muscle and his teeth were wide. Whenever he smiled, many single women hoped they would be the one to catch his eye.

He wanted nothing to do with them. He refused to be promised to the pretty ones, the strong ones, even the ones who might enhance connections between tribes. His younger brothers had already married and a few had even made him an uncle. It wasn't that he wasn't interested in marriage. But he wanted only the young dancer.

Whenever he saw her, his heart squeezed into a tight little stone. *You'll marry me,* he thought. Yet doubt filled up his chest and left little room for breath or blood. He would have given up his muscles and his smile, he would have traded away all his skills for that one woman. The two were very similar in that way. Both were consumed by a passion for only one thing.

Oh, how the bachelor tried to woo the beautiful dancer. He played the didgeridoo while she danced. After every hunt he took the choicest meats to her mother. He even traded with the desert tribes for ochre and painted his body with the symbols of love magic. None of it worked. Although the woman treated him kindly, she would not make a place in her life for him.

He became frustrated...very frustrated. Soon he'd had enough of wooing and romance and magic. He decided to steal her away. He would force himself on her and make her become his wife. She could still dance...after she gave birth to the babies and gathered the family's food and captured small game for their daily meals and cooked the meat of the large animals he would occasionally kill....*then* she could dance as much as she liked.

And so he made a handful of strong, accurate spears. He bound sharp stones to the ends of fighting sticks. He selected his best club, the one made of ironwood, and tied it to his belt. The whole clan might defend her so he had to be ready. It was also possible that another man might ambush him later. What he stole could be stolen. He would kill to keep her.

He was ready. The girl had been dancing all night, so she and her family would soon be asleep. If he did everything right, the pair would be deep in the bush before anyone realized the dancer was missing. He stashed the spears along his escape route so both hands would be free to capture the lovely young woman.

The wind spirits happened to brush against the bachelor just then. They immediately knew his intention. If he succeeded, the tribe would lose an important source of joy. The spirits rushed back to find the woman still dancing at the edge of the fire's light. Everyone else was asleep. No one would witness her capture, no one would be able to save her. Only the wind spirits could prevent the tragedy, and even that could only be done one way.

They brushed over her twirling, twisting body. They painted her skin with invisible ochre and whispered magic words. Her lungs pulled hard at every breath. She'd never felt so willowy and supple, her legs had never felt so long. Throwing back her head, she shut her eyes and spun in the shadows. She did not see how her body was changing; she felt only the ecstasy of becoming.

The bachelor crept through the camp. None of the sleeping forms were the prize he sought. *Perhaps she has already been stolen,* he thought as anger gripped his throat. Then he spotted her in the shadows. Of course! She would dance until she dropped into the cool, dark dreams where love made her truly happy. When it was done, when he had forced her to become his wife, she would realize he was right. She would have it all...and he would have her.

He lunged. Just then, the magic whispers fell silent. The dancer's arms had become wings and her long neck and legs made her as tall as any man. Before the bachelor could grab her, the wind lifted her beyond his reach. She had become the brolga, a steel-blue crane that dances its joyful courtship in the marsh.

The Message of The Dance

True transcendence occurs when passion and creativity lead you to your divine self. No suitor or elder or friend can force you to become that which you are not meant to be. Only you can decide to dance on the winds that support you, only you can connect with the spirits and energies that will shape-shift you into new life.

In this story, a young woman was promised the best marriage, a dedicated husband, and all the support a mother could want for her family. But that vision belonged to people who believed that a satisfying life looked like everyone else's. If she had accepted the mainstream version of happiness, she would not have been able to express her joy. The usual trappings of bliss would not have brought her any pleasure.

People are as individual as river rocks. Not everyone will be happy in the deepest current, the lifestyle defined as normal. Even when a goal is only somewhat unusual, there is still pressure to perfectly fit the mold. If you are one of those unique individuals, you must dedicate yourself to achieving what is best for you. What you sacrifice won't matter. As long as you feel passion, you will also feel joy.

The key is transformation…spiritual, mental and physical. You might remain single, have fewer children or take a sabbatical. You might move, go back to school or switch careers. At every step you will be guided by the best compass people have, passion. Passion will point the way to the contribution only you can make. It will bring you back to yourself.

Even when others disbelieve, even when they talk about you and to you as if your passion could easily be turned to other pursuits, you must hold true to yourself. Not everyone has the courage to start their own journey. Once begun, the journey requires extraordinary strength just to stay the course. When people try to saddle you with their own limits, thank them for speaking their truth and recognize that those limits are not your own.

When you transform, you will feel the ecstasy of becoming. You will bless the world with gifts no other living being can offer. Along the way, avoid the shadow side. Since no one was courageous or outrageous enough to be the dancer's friend, mentor or true lover, she was dangerously isolated. Her passion became a dark undertow. Left in human form, she would have danced herself to death.

The bachelor had already been swept away by his own rip current. He adored the young woman yet he did not really love her. No one did. They loved her energy, her beauty and grace; they loved the pleasure she brought them when she danced her own joy. But they could not truly love her because they did not believe that her passion was real. If they had, their love would have transcended mainstream expectations.

Today public and private schools squelch a child's natural ability in order to create a well-rounded individual. By producing adults with many opportunities for a modest level of success, passion is stunted or eliminated. From cradle to grave, those who would follow their hearts must break rules and overstep boundaries. Only the bravest and strongest...or the wealthiest...ever get the chance.

To allow everyone the opportunity to transcend, we must recognize that expectations are nothing more than guidelines. They can create pathways for people who are floundering but should never become prisons. Individuals who veer off for a while or for a lifetime are our entrepreneurs and our geniuses, our small business owners and our Einsteins. When individuals follow their dreams, they benefit everyone.

No one offered the dancer that freedom or support. They could not transform themselves enough to reach beyond society's expectations. They did not have her vision; they loved only how her exquisite sacrifice brought them joy. They meant the best for her, of course. But in pressuring her to follow the common path, they pushed her further into the shadows.

Perhaps the bachelor felt her slipping into the darkness. Perhaps his subconscious knew she must connect with society to avoid being lost. He could have married without expecting children or he might have loved her as a friend. Despite his wealth of abilities, though, he lacked creativity. He was as unsuited to the task as the dancer had become to her community.

The pair represents extremes. The blending of their lives could have enabled them to remain unique and to uniquely benefit their tribe. But the bachelor's sheer excellence at what was expected of a man blinded him to anything except what was expected of a woman. Because he couldn't imagine a relationship that fell outside the norm, he chose a path that threatened them both.

In thinking he could force her to be his wife, he failed to respect the fullness of what she might have given freely. In plotting to kidnap her, he planned to steal a source of joy from his tribe. By preparing to kill any who might defend her or steal her from his own arms, he proved himself willing to destroy the people who loved her. In the end, he failed himself. Once she was gone, what woman could ever stir his passion?

The wind spirits saved the dancer from the misery the bachelor sought to impose as well as the misery she was creating for herself. We achieve our full potential only when we interact with a larger community. Her single-minded path threatened to tumble her beyond the light of her tribe. Even the most beautiful dance performed alone would not have prevented an important part of her humanity from being destroyed.

When she transformed into an entirely new species, her humanity ceased to be an issue. The transformation also benefited the people she left behind. While even an astonishing dancer might eventually be forgotten, brolgas continue to bring humans joy. Her descendents remind us that passion is as important to our lives as reproduction is to our species.

This is the gleaming side of transformation. This is the message sent to us from the Dreamtime. When we pursue our passion, when we generate our own bliss, we spread our joy to everyone around us. Dance your dream into life and you dance for us all.

Thirst

Tiddalick was an average kind of frog. During the wet season, he hopped around eating bugs. He was never far from a cool billabong. As the dry season set in and waterholes shrank, the frog buried himself in the mud. For weeks and months he didn't move. Only when the monsoon rain trickled down to his hideaway did he come out again.

One morning Tiddalick awoke with a powerful thirst. The dry season was coming and he needed to prepare his underground home. But on this day, the knowledge of the thirst to come was a torment. It seemed like all the thirst he'd felt his entire life had returned at once. He could think of nothing else...not the soft mouthful a grub made nor the prickly bundle of fly legs on his tongue. There was only the memory of his terrible thirst.

He hopped to the edge of a lake and began to drink. He gulped down gallons but still he was thirty, still he imagined the torment of that annual hardship. He kept drinking until the lake went dry. Although his belly was quite swollen, Tiddalick moved straight to a river. Water rushed and roared and gurgled down his throat until the river also ran dry.

By then the frog had ballooned to enormous proportions. He had also attracted a crowd of birds and animals. At first they ridiculed Tiddalick and his absurd thirst. Soon, though, they realized they were all in danger. If he didn't stop, he would drink the country dry. Everyone except the frog would die.

They tried all sorts of things to make him stop. They told him stories about sharing and fairness. When that didn't work, they fussed and frowned and sent the elder council to shame him.

They even tried threats. Everyone knew they were empty, though. Tiddalick was already as big as Uluru, that giant stone in the middle of the desert. No one could force him to do anything.

Tiddalick drank and drank and drank. He sucked up every puddle and stream, he lapped up all the soaks. He inhaled the tiny pools atop flat boulders. When the last drop had disappeared, when every creek bed lay parched, the frog couldn't move. He didn't mind, though. At last…at last!…his thirst had been quenched.

The animals waited for him to wiggle his toes or scratch his belly. The movement might make him burp a little water. They couldn't wait long, though, because the heat was already taking its toll. Then Kangaroo had an idea. If they could make the frog laugh, his mouth would open wide. The shaking of his belly would push the water up his throat. Surely whole lakes would spill out.

Kangaroo tried all kinds of tricks to make him laugh. She spun on her tail and hopped in crazy zigzags but Tiddalick didn't even smile. Willy Wagtail and Cockatoo stepped in with their own type of clowning. They dove at each other and fell to the ground with exaggerated screams. When their frenzy reached its peak, Tiddalick simply closed his eyes.

The country fell silent. The animals were lost.

Then Kookaburra began to sing her strange, stuttering call. The sound was like a chuckle that built to a rattling laugh. It clattered against rocks and echoed back from the cliffs. Her glee was as relentless as Tiddalick's thirst, as irresistible as the wind. Despite their predicament, the animals couldn't help but laugh.

The sound was infectious. Tiddalick's mouth twitched. He squeezed shut his eyes and pinched in his cheeks but a smile tugged at his mouth. He was smiling! Kookaburra threw out endless peals while Tiddalick's face stayed frozen in that strangled joy. For a long moment, Kookaburra feared she would fail.

Then Tiddalick's skin began to ripple. Finally…finally!…he opened his wide mouth. *Ho, ha, ha!* he boomed. *He, ha, ho!*

Water gushed as high as the sun. It splashed back down into the dry riverbeds and ran as crystal streams. The billabongs were cool once more, precious caches could again be found in deep crevices and atop flat rocks. Tiddalick shrank back to his normal size and never bothered the animals again.

His descendents still suffer that terrible thirst. Before disappearing into their burrows, they store extra water in their bladders. In an emergency, people who know where to dig can squeeze the frog until it gives them a drink of water.

The Message of Thirst

Although this story seems to teach a simple lesson about greed, the message for modern readers is very different. Tiddalick survived many dry seasons before he drank up all the water. He suffered during previous entombments yet always emerged healthy and alive. His new craving far surpassed any survival instinct. Tiddalick's thirst became an addiction.

To understand this message, forget about alcohol and prescription painkillers, meth, cocaine, heroin, and every other drug abused in our society. Those substances are so laden with grief it's difficult to recognize that they are not the actual cause of addiction. The real driver is found in the psyche.

Tiddalick's need sprang from fear. Because his behavior originated with a feeling, it couldn't be quelled by logic. The powerful thirsts we face today are also rooted in our emotions. We feel a near-obsessive need for many things—food to replace the comfort we used to find in communities and relationships, wealth to leverage the status that used to accrue through generosity, and thrilling electronics that distract us from the hard work of dealing with our issues.

Food, money, talking heads and TV shows aren't the problem. Nor are they the solution. Unfortunately, we turn to them for solace so often they become a different kind of drug. Eventually the flood of information and entertainment from televisions, computers and smartphones creates an addiction to more. More updates, more excitement, more spinning colors and flashing lights...just more.

Embedded in that flood are thirty-second clips geared to turn other modest thirsts into addictions. The average TV show contains eighteen minutes of commercials per hour. In eighteen minutes, you could lift weights or call a friend. You could cook a healthy meal or stroll around the neighborhood. Multiply that by the average number of viewing hours per day and advertisements get ample opportunity to make us crave what we do not have and probably do not need.

The internet isn't much better. Most of its offerings are bits that can be scanned rather than read. They are meant to be consumed like popcorn, one after the other, each a pleasing moment that vaporizes as quickly as it is tasted. This bombardment isn't ruining our brains. Instead, the problem is that our brains are hardwired for a primitive version of Twitter. A look at our social evolution proves it.

In our earliest centuries, humans formed societies of hunters and gatherers. Stalking animals and finding food required us to scan wide sections of the landscape. Our minds had to process vast quantities of information quickly: pick out signs that predators or enemies hid nearby; identify edible plants and easy game; assess an area's potential to meet current and future needs.

The process ended with a judgment. A specific plant or animal was selected. When we honed in on that single thing, our focus shifted from broad to pinpoint...just as it does when we select one show or article from the information landscape. And here is where electronic wizardry confounds our minds and our emotions.

Whereas the hunter-gatherer spent considerable time focused on a chosen task—gather berries, stalk emu—modern man has far fewer opportunities for prolonged focus. Commercials interrupt too often, internet feeds are too short, and multitasking is considered more important than fully engaging in a single activity. We are encouraged to become jacks-of-all-trades and masters of none.

We also miss out on the usual reward. We don't receive the endorphin rush that comes from thrusting home a spear or carrying a basket heavy with bush tucker. An electronic experience does not engage the sense of smell, taste or touch. While new virtual attachments can simulate touch, we still end up with no tangible benefit. The only thing left is the input itself. We become addicted not to the stimulus but to *the process of searching for the stimulus.*

We become like gamblers. Brain imaging studies have shown that gambling addicts are not hooked on winning but on the anticipation they feel while they play. For them, winning is substantially less thrilling than hoping to win. Constantly losing, which allows players to constantly anticipate winning, is therefore more satisfying than hitting the jackpot.

The mechanism of gambling addiction sounds backwards and it is. It defies logic because its intense pleasure is more immediately rewarding than any cost-benefit analysis of finances or time. In our electronic world, every click of the mouse or the remote control is a roll of digitized dice. The hand we are dealt, the web page or TV program we find, demands that we switch into a more focused state of mind. The rewards of this circuitry are more meditative in nature and therefore take longer to kick in. It is much easier to roll again, to click to another site or keep surfing the channels.

The catch is that any kind of repetitive input can change brain chemistry. The system adapts, usually by creating more receptors for the "feel good" chemicals produced by that activity. When those receptors are left empty because the stimulus of alcohol, surfing, drugs or gambling has been removed, the pain of withdrawal is as much physical as it is emotional.

The story's message about thirst, then, is especially important today. Millions of people have access to food, money and material goods in quantities unheard of only generations ago. Our modern environment also challenges our ability to adapt in a healthy way. When we buy cars that can go twice the legal speed limit and the rush of surfing can be topped only by appearing on TV, we have built an entire culture on the quest for an addictive rush.

Staying on the right side of that line can be difficult. Every day we engage in potentially addictive activities that are nonetheless necessary to our survival. Eating and sunbathing both stimulate the release of endorphins. It's nature's way of ensuring that we regularly nourish our bodies and create vitamin D. But when performed at extreme levels, eating and sunbathing turn deadly.

We ridiculed the idea that video games could be addictive until brain scans proved otherwise. We ignored the relentless assault on childhood by television viewing time until the obesity epidemic struck our youth. We dismiss the impact of email and social networking until our servers go down and we wander like ghosts through our own lives.

The only thing that can oppose the insecurity and self-importance driving our thirst is the infinitely more powerful force of joy. Fear and addiction catch people in a tight embrace. They become immobile, inflexible and unable to give. Joy is like Kookaburra's infectious laugh. Joy is the heart's true vibration, the energy that pours from us when we achieve harmony. When joy appears, even an addict can change.

SEVEN SISTERS

    Real joy isn't found by surfing input like a crack-addicted lab rat pushes a dispensing button. The most realistic CG world coupled with a full kinetic suit can't replace the complexity of human interaction. As much as we enjoy or even need to indulge in certain experiences, we will never feel true joy if we do not conquer our thirst.

    Remember that the dry season is always followed by the quenching rains; likewise, the drought of our souls will always be followed by an abundance of joy. Our thirsts need to be controlled because even those things that seem absurd can do a lot of damage. When we manage our desires, even someone whose role seems as insignificant as that of a tiny frog can quench another's thirst.

Trickery

Baiame, the lead sky spirit, arranged the world in a special way. He mixed certain animals with people in the desert regions and other animals with people along the coast. He divided saltwater fish from those that swam only in fresh water, and he sent insects to live in the trees and earth and air.

Women he set aside on their own. He scattered men across the continent except for the women's land; he made homes for animals in every habitat except with the women. Never would a fang tear their flesh, never would a spine sting their feet. They would know only good health all their long lives and would raise their children in absolute safety.

Yet Baiame never intended for men and women to avoid each other. The women needed meat and skins from the animals the men hunted. The men needed the extraordinary tools and weapons crafted by the women. Other things were also traded...gifts, glances, flirtations. Although men and women went their separate ways each evening, those flirtatious looks served their purpose.

After years of peace and prosperity, one man decided he didn't like having to barter every time he lost a boomerang or broke a spear. And perhaps he didn't like having to provide a fair trade value for other things, either. At any rate, he said that men should not pander to women by trading with them as equals. Instead, they should force the women to provide for them.

An elder waved the notion away as if it were a pesky fly. If they forced the women to work, surely the quality of their crafts would fall. Inferior weapons would make hunting less efficient. If the men spent more time away from camp, they wouldn't be able to carry water or build fires. Their lives would be worse, not better.

The rebel said the women could be forced to perform all the extra chores. The elder called him a fool. Women who were busy hauling water and tending camp wouldn't have time to make weapons. Then no one would hunt. All the wood and water in the country wouldn't put food in their bellies.

The rebel's tongue would not be still. He talked of stealing the women's tools, of men carving their own woomeras and hardening their own spears. Most of the others dismissed his ranting...but not all. Some men felt the same resentment or saw nothing wrong with enslaving women. They respected the weapons more than the people who made them.

The rebel and his new friends formed a plan. For several days, they corralled animals in gullies near where the women lived. Then they gathered frogs and snakes and lizards in large sacks. They wove giant nets to capture flocks of birds. They even plucked ants from their mounds and nabbed mosquitoes from the air.

Finally they stood together on a hill. The morning was new and the women were coaxing the embers of their fires back to life. A brilliant red glow in the east predicted a dry, hot day. Soon the sun glinted off a lake next to the women's camp. The men waited for just the right moment to unleash their trickery.

The rebel began to conjure. He knew the powerful words that named things and brought them into being. As he sang, he mixed pipe clay with water and rubbed the paste on his two brothers. Their legs shrank and their feet splayed. Their bodies grew plump while their necks stretched as long as a spear. When the white clay dried, it turned into a layer of fluffy feathers. The brothers had become swans.

They flew to the lake and landed on the shimmering water. The women had never seen such enchanting creatures before.

Every able-bodied woman launched a canoe. They would surround the lovely birds and coax them onto their land.

While the women were distracted, the men stole into their camp. They took all the tools—the long sticks used to break spinifex grass and extract its sticky resin, strips of kangaroo sinew for tying up woomeras, and stone chips used as blades in fighting clubs. They even gathered up embers in case the flames used to harden spears were different than the men's cooking fires.

When the women spotted the thieves, they shouted war cries and paddled hard for shore. As they landed, the men released the animals. Kangaroos and wallabies fled in a panic. Thousands of snakes turned the earth into a writhing skein. Birds and beetles and mosquitoes flew up like monsoon rains returning to the skies.

Just as the rebel had hoped, the women scattered. They could make tools anytime but had never been able to hunt. If they could catch just a few animals, they wouldn't have to trade with the men as much. They could also demand more for the things they did trade. Soon both sides were back in their camps with their newfound treasures.

The women enjoyed the cockatoos dancing in their trees and the tiny hills pebble-mound mice built at their feet. The men practiced with the tools and eventually made weapons nearly as well as the women. Both sides took pleasure in not having to barter. And since they still flirted with each other, the raid didn't seem to have done any real harm.

As time passed, though, the elder was proven right. With all the extra work they were doing, neither side could keep up with the chores. When some of the women began to stay with their lovers in the men's camp, they discovered that dividing the chores returned their former quality of life. Soon men and women lived together in every part of the world.

Baiame allowed these changes but had to punish the rebel. Since the man's brothers had been the instruments that confounded the original creation, they would also be the instruments of the rebel's grief. Baiame sent an eagle to rip out the swans' feathers. The bewitched pair began to sink. The rebel couldn't swim fast enough to help them and his magic wasn't powerful enough to fight off an eagle. His brothers would drown.

A flock of crows flew over to investigate the commotion. Long ago, they had also rebelled against Baiame so they decided to help the brothers. While a few distracted the eagle, the rest carried the swans to dry land. By then the pair had feathers only on the tips of their wings. Each crow gave up a few of its own feathers to clothe them. Ever since, Australian swans have been black with white wing tips.

The Message of Trickery

Nowadays the chores, duties and ceremonies of men, called men's business, are less often separated from women's business. Even in industrialized societies, though, holdovers from earlier times still linger. Although these divisions have been used to oppress certain groups, it's important to recognize why the separation used to be beneficial.

People can survive without any division of labor. But survival at a minimal level doesn't meet humanity's greater need for art, music, philosophy and celebration. Ironically, recent presidential administrations that forcefully stumped for family and social values viciously cut programs that nurtured those values. A country devoid of art and philosophy and leisure, no matter how advanced its technology, degenerates into a survival mentality.

Since survival mentalities are necessarily harsh, societies that lack creative outlets or that restrict creative outlets to the wealthy are often hyper-violent, intolerant, religiously oppressive, or lack basic human rights. Worldwide, the level of domestic violence increases in families with fewer opportunities for leisure activities or spontaneity. Then and now, the division of labor can address the issue.

In ancient times, chores were not divided only by gender. Elders counseled the tribe while young adults performed chores that required more physical stamina than skill. Children gathered bush tucker while couples in their prime raised families. In modern societies, labor laws focus a child's time on education. Seniors start second careers. And as the childbearing years have expanded, young adults pursue college degrees and challenging careers before starting a family.

When men and women lived in their own territories and divided labor by creating different trade items, they enjoyed a lifestyle above a survival level. The women had time to appreciate beauty, which is why the swans distracted them. The men clearly enjoyed their lives because the rebel could only coax a handful of others to join him. Both genders were comfortable, they lived the way Baiame had decreed, they lived well. But did they live well enough?

This Aboriginal Garden of Eden had the same issues as the Christian paradise. Every physical need had been met yet the mind, its creativity and its genius, was trapped in a perfect stasis. A society entrenched in its belief in divine order can grow only if it is willing to punch through the status quo. The rebel did exactly that. Despite being driven by insecurity and selfishness, he served a larger purpose.

His attitude wasn't terribly enlightened yet it was common enough. We still think of people we don't know as *other:* foreign, unconsecrated, uneducated or ill informed, different, bizarre, uncouth, misled or evil. Races, cultures and subcultures, generations and genders and professions divide our species. We even have different politics, a trait common in every monkey troop and lion pride that can reach ridiculous extremes when paired with mankind's higher reasoning.

This chaos of divisions and extremes creates a paradise of opportunity. Only by reuniting in an utterly new way could the Aboriginal society remake itself. After joining together, couples grew closer and families became stronger. If people were better off after the chaos, though, why had women been set apart in the first place? Had Baiame made a mistake?

Apparently he was thinking ahead. Humans need to learn their own lessons even if they suffer in the process. Eve lifted mankind out of an animalistic mindset by eating the fruit of knowledge; Athena embodied wisdom by bursting from Zeus' head. If Baiame had assigned men and women their own business right from the start, people would not have understood the benefits. Since we reject what we do not understand, our intellectual evolution would have been stunted. The rebel was as necessary to humanity as the biblical serpent.

Humanity is now in the midst of another transformation. Our population has grown large enough to specialize based on skill and desire. Men and women of every age and race are crossing boundaries and creating new opportunities. Allowing women to take positions of power and men to fulfill nurturing roles supercharges our social evolution. Powerful women and loving men make our nation strong.

What holds true for man's law holds true for spiritual law. In Aboriginal society, ritual and ceremony were also separated into men's business and women's business. Anthropological records lack information about women' spiritual lives because the male anthropologists were forbidden to see those rites. Since the European visitors allowed only men to be spiritual leaders, they assumed that Aboriginal women had no role.

For centuries now, women in many modern societies have been shut out of spiritual roles. Countries suffer when governments do not hear the voices of every citizen. Our hearts suffer when we do not connect with both male and female energies. As more religions clear a path to the pulpit for women, the resonance of our hearts changes. We ascend to higher planes. We evolve in mind and soul.

We have taken great strides in unlocking doors for women, yet the same dynamic holds back other groups. White-collar workers could not dedicate their lives to intellectual pursuits if blue-collar workers didn't build houses and pour asphalt and drive big rigs. Every worker must be valued as highly as any other.

All of this evolution and transformation and change can seem as chaotic as wild animals overrunning our home. But there is a purpose to the process. There is also a difference between calling for something to appear and taking action to make sure it arrives. Even the most ethereal butterfly must build its chrysalis, and sometimes rebels must rise up against the establishment.

Day by day we are dismantling the old status quo. In its place we build a society that is flexible, tolerant and free. As we continue dividing our labor in new ways, we must recognize that all skills lift us further from survival mode. In this way spiritual, mental and financial benefits accrue to us all. In this way we follow the true divine decree: to live well together.

Yandying

Long ago, the world was shrouded in a perpetual dusk. No sun or moon shone like beacons. The only light came from the stars, the campfires lit by the sky spirits. People living on Earth built their own fires to cut through the gloom.

Hunting was very difficult. The men had special boomerangs, large weapons carved so that one side was shorter than the other. These boomerangs didn't return and were used to stun animals. The weapons didn't help much, though. The men rarely brought home any meat.

The darkness created different problems for the women. They couldn't spot flying birds, so finding nests with their tasty eggs was difficult. The women also never knew when lizards or snakes might be resting. A lot of effort was wasted digging up empty burrows. And since plants didn't grow very quickly, large areas had to be covered to find enough fruit and seeds.

As time passed, the tribes stripped every stick of firewood from the land. People spent more time looking for wood, which meant they had less time to look for food. Neighboring tribes became a threat. Raids for food and wood became frequent. Soon only the most experienced hunters were allowed to stand watch. Only they could tell whether movement in the bush was the wind or a stalking enemy.

That left only younger, less experienced men to hunt, and that meant even less meat than before. People began to argue over the smallest thing. A missing scrap of food or an imagined slight could start a fistfight. Teenagers hid their fears behind disobedience and elders threw insults. One experienced hunter studied these developments with despair.

This darkness is like a weight, he thought. *Soon it will darken our souls.*

He watched a woman sitting near a fire with a coolamon, an oblong wood bowl. She was cleaning native millet seeds by shaking sand and dust to the bottom of the bowl. When the seeds formed a layer on top, a tap of just the right force separated that layer from the dirt.

The process, called yandying, required patience and skill. But native millet could be gathered easily from the ground and for now kept the tribe alive. Although the work was painstaking, the woman rarely looked up. She yandied enough to grind into a few cakes, then several. Given time, she would yandy the harvest of a broad plain.

The hunter couldn't bear to watch so much effort being wasted on such a tiny reward. He ran straight past the watchmen and deep into the bush. Even when he spotted enemy scouts, he didn't stop. He ran until his throat was torn by the dusk and his eyes were boggled by gloom. When he could run no further, he batted the air as if the darkness could be broken like spider's silk.

The dusk was driving his people into starvation, cruelty and fear. There had to be an answer, one that didn't rely on women yandying away their lives. Then his breath stopped. He replayed the woman's every move in his mind: the gentle swirling and tapping that shifted the dust to the bottom, the firm bump that separated the layers. The same movements again. And again.

The pile had grown...slowly, yes, but eventually enough to make a meal. Determination and skill had turned slag into nutritious cakes. Surely her back had ached and her legs had fallen asleep yet her efforts had gathered one thing from the other. She had found food among the chaff.

All during the hunter's life, his tribe had thought the dusk was an impossible burden. It served no purpose except to confound; it seemed as useless as chaff and as abundant as dust. Now he saw that light and darkness were mixed just like the seeds were mixed with the dirt. What if he could separate the dusk into its different parts? What if he could yandy light from the darkness?

He ran back to camp and woke the woman. He stoked the fire back to life and handed her a coolamon. The intensity of his focus was a tangible force more powerful than words. She understood that what he wanted was more important than sleep. Although the pair had not spoken, she resumed her work.

He sat absolutely still. Even as the mosquitoes drained his blood, even when the camp dogs sniffed his hands, he did not move. He watched her shake apart the layers, *tap-tap-swoosh.* He watched her shift the layer of seeds, *shhk!* He heard the patter of the millet atop the grinding rock and the splash of dirt pitched from the coolamon.

When the camp began to wake, the woman's eyes were hollow from fatigue. As long as the hunter watched, though, she would work. Their friends stopped by to chat but the pair remained lost in their own world. Children gathered to watch. The elders thought surely the hunter would take the woman for his wife.

The woman kept yandying, *tap, swoosh, shhk!* Her sisters came now and then to bring her more seeds and to grind the clean ones. Occasionally the woman wiped her forehead or brushed away a fly; otherwise she was locked in a trance with the hunter. Even the shamans would not interfere. The yandying continued through all the waking hours then longer as the children shut their tired eyes.

It was impossible. Even if the hunter could gather the dusk into a coolamon, all the tribes in the world could never winnow enough light to make a difference. Even if they could, the light would be in separate piles and no better than a campfire.

Still he watched. He matched the woman's patience, he watched her repetitive actions while his mind expanded. Eventually he focused on the moment when the top layer shifted. The movement was firm yet controlled. His muscles used that same precise power when he threw a boomerang. He imagined the swirling spin of the weapon and felt it cutting the wind.

He stood abruptly and walked into the bush. While the woman watched, he searched for the perfect wood. He carved four giant boomerangs, the kind that didn't return, then painted them white on top and black on the bottom. The whole time, he sang a yandying song. The magic of his words was strong. The wood fairly shook with power.

He threw the boomerangs to the east and the west, the south and the north. They flew straight and true, spinning always with the white side on top and the black side on the bottom. There was a mighty *shhk!* as darkness pooled on one side of the earth and light gathered on the other. The sun and moon coalesced and settled into position. To this day, they give the planet light and dark at the proper times.

The Message of Yandying

Every day we are pitted against dark situations in our lives and within our souls. The dusk can drown our humanity, our compassion and our patience. Like the hunter, we take on internal quests in order to generate external changes. When we seek the light, though, we must remember not to eliminate the darkness.

At the end of this story, darkness and light had been separated yet remained whole. Each had something important to contribute, so neither could be destroyed in favor of the other. Too much light would have damaged the environment as much as too little light. Both had to be given a place in the world.

When dark and light were mixed, they could not serve their separate purposes. The only way people could survive in that situation was to pressure the environment. When the natural world began to break down, human society also began to break down. The story obviously teaches balance between man and nature, a message as important today as it was in ancient times. What isn't so obvious is the message that the environment itself must sometimes change.

Nowadays, we occasionally blame environmental problems on technology or greed when the real issue is about survival and change. In the story, the environment pressured the tribe into pressuring the environment. The perpetual dusk forced them to burn every available bit of wood and debris that otherwise would have nurtured new plants. The dusk inhibited plant growth so people stripped off fruit and vegetables before the seeds could mature. By fighting off immediate starvation, they guaranteed future starvation.

Our world faces the same challenges today. People in South America don't want their rainforests to be replaced by plowed fields; nor do they want their children to starve. Haiti's earthquake survivors didn't loot for eight days because they were greedy. Even the resources consumed by crisis relief organizations can be as environmentally expensive as the disaster. All these activities are stopgaps until we can implement changes that ensure long-term survival.

Humans are the only holistic-minded species on Earth. Our planet is concerned with plate shifts, magnetic fields and ocean currents. Sometimes its movements disrupt the localized worlds of humans, plants and animals. Changing our actions won't stop a hurricane or calm a tsunami. Sometimes we must use the strength of the hunter and the patience of the yandying woman to change the world.

It's far from simple. When our planet or our situation shifts profoundly, the accepted wisdom becomes useless. That's why the elder council couldn't solve the problem of dusk. Although their experience was broad and deep, the council was limited to what its members had seen during their lives. Modern leaders also become mired in what has failed or succeeded in the past. It's difficult to find a new path when judgments are branded into our thought patterns.

On some level the elders knew change was necessary. They adjusted the traditions associated with hunting and watch duty yet they missed the mark. They changed human behavior when they should have changed their way of thinking. Humans tend to modify everything around a problem in order to cope, to tolerate, to survive a little longer. We hope for radical change even when we suspect it cannot come from the entrenched administration.

Before we can move forward, at least one of us has to change radically. Only a visionary, often someone outside the establishment, can set aside what is known and leap into the unknown. This is the playground of children and shamans. Imagination flows freely in a mind that is free from the past. Trance work, prayer and meditation eliminate the judgments that blight seed concepts before they can bloom.

Even this process requires that opposites be given their rightful places. Divine inspiration is a blend of logic and intuition. The intuitive flow allows the mind to roam a universe of potential until the answer explodes in an inspired flash. The complexity of our brains allows us to see through the tangle and find the single thread that needs to be plucked.

This Aboriginal story is a perfect example of the process. The hunter knew that yandying the dusk was impossible. He allowed the repetitive nature of the woman's work, the absolute stillness of his own body, and even the sounds of yandying to narrow his attention. The pinpoint focus pushed him into a trance where his mind could merge with the universal flow.

How the hunter came to the trance state is also important. His run through the bush, although triggered by frustration, prepared him for the trance. Only after his body was exhausted did his mind surrender to the intuitive flow. The woman's willingness to maintain her trancelike movement supported the hunter's mental yandying. His quest was internal yet he was not alone in his quest.

Perhaps the most powerful message springs from the couple's humanity, both their fragility and their power. The hunter and the woman were average people with no special abilities beyond what any person might achieve. The tribe did not understand their odd behavior but because they engaged in it together, they were left alone. Together they reached a level of consciousness far removed from everyday thought. When the hunter took that new knowledge and imbued his physical actions with spiritual intent, he implemented a mystical solution in the physical realm.

To successfully face our modern challenges, we must stop adjusting everything around an issue. We go green with our technology when a German Shepherd's carbon footprint is three times larger than an SUV's. We complain about national healthcare's flaws when lack of coverage guarantees suffering. Like the hunter, we must break through our institutionalized wisdom and search for the cosmic solution. We must make the impossible possible.

When we take this leap, we recognize that darkness cannot be discarded. Nor can we expect opposites to blend without creating a new problem, a different kind of dusk. Instead, opposites must be given their own place in the world. Physical force fails without spiritual intent. Men and women must pool their special abilities. When we honor the opposites, we create lasting success.

Perpetual dusk, the constant presence of different challenges, has been our burden since we formed our first coherent thought. We are not here to create coping mechanisms that are more destructive than the dusk. We are here to find the proper place for darkness so we can fully appreciate its opposite. We must not mistake light for the sole solution least we burn up in its heat.

The darkest of our impulses, both as individuals and as societies, reveal our greatest potential. We walk in the light knowing night will eventually fall; we wait in the darkness knowing the sun will eventually rise. During those dusky transitions when energies change, we must free our spirits to travel past our minds.

When we return from the journey into soul space, we must create our power tools in the material world. We must imbue those tools and our actions with spiritual intent. Then we must yandy our dusk. If we do not, we guarantee our own starvation. We will cause as much harm as an enemy invader.

When we settle our light and our darkness into their rightful places, each of us becomes a galaxy of thought and intention, logic and spirit. We orbit around each other in harmony. After earthquakes and tsunamis, we grow by building on the best of the old and allowing the rest to fall away. Always we return to our own axes, wobbling a bit yet balanced, to share our magnetic energy with the universe of humanity.

The Glow

Moon had a body that was large and round, as if he spent all his time feasting. His arms and legs were spindly things that stuck out every which way like spinifex grass. With a shape like that, he wasn't much good at running or jumping or hunting. He was good at one thing...or so he claimed. According to the women he'd charmed, his promises were much more exciting than his performance.

Moon stayed a bachelor all his life. Not every young person found a mate right away but single men had plenty of ways to make themselves useful. They hunted meat for their clan and participated in men's ceremonies. They made clubs and spears and woomeras, simple devices that propelled their spears much farther. And there were always brothers or cousins or nephews to guide.

None of that was important to Moon. He didn't care about marriage, and he certainly didn't want the responsibility that came with raising children. He just wanted to touch women, to be with them for one night. Then they could marry any man they chose; he, meanwhile, would woo the next young lady.

Poor, poor Moon. Such ambitions belonged to better men, and his silvery words failed more often than they succeeded.

The women had all been warned about him. His crafty tongue could sing such beautiful words that inexperienced girls couldn't help but swoon. So they avoided him as if he were a cannibal; they wouldn't even look at him for fear of falling under his spell. No matter how hard Moon tried, he usually couldn't get close enough to a woman to talk to her.

His failures dragged at him like a river in flood. Soon he became so bitter no one wanted to be around him. Not his friends or other bachelors, not his uncles or cousins...and certainly not women. Whenever he appeared, all the ladies hid in their *gunyahs,* huts made of tree bark. His desire was too palpable, his lust too ravenous. Surely even peeking through a crack at him would curse a woman with twins.

Every evening Moon walked along the stony ridges. He preferred the high ground so that people—especially the ladies—could see him. He kept his giant, round body oiled with emu fat. His skin glowed so brilliantly it lit up the earth. Every night he paraded about hoping to attract flocks of lovely, eager women. If he failed to attract attention, he made sure to use more emu fat the next night.

One evening he descended into a valley to visit a shallow stream. Although a deep river lay just over the ridge, he never went near the rushing water. He couldn't swim and was afraid of falling in. So he gazed at his reflection in the stream, turning this way and that to admire the smoothness of his skin and the brightness of his glow.

When he was finally done feasting on his image, he climbed up onto the ridge. He was surprised to see two attractive women by the river. Since his light had been hidden by the valley, they hadn't known to run away. It seemed that his luck was about to change.

The women watched him approach. They knew that if Moon got to talking, one of them might not go home that night. But they were closer to him now than they had ever been. His gleaming skin was indeed bright. But was it really as smooth as it seemed? Just this once they decided not to run away.

Ah, Moon thought, *they are captivated by my rugged strength. Ah,* he thought, *they will fall into my sheltering arms!*

He didn't seem to hear their giggles. When he was close enough for them to make out his brittle twig legs and his soft, round body and his spindly spinifex arms, they jumped into their canoes. He broke into a waddling run as they pushed off with their paddles.

Apparently they, like all the women, were intimidated by his immensely handsome face. He wanted both of them so badly his spiny little fingers twitched. They were too far away to reach with his hands but he could still reach them with his words. In a voice as pleasantly smooth as his skin, he asked if they would ferry him across the river.

The women talked it over and agreed to help. But they would not sit in the canoe with him; even they were not that adventurous. They both got into the smaller craft then pushed the empty one up on the bank. As Moon wedged his massive torso inside, the canoe drifted into the current. He panicked and cried for help in a reedy, piping voice more like a frog than a man. The women rolled their eyes.

He can't paddle, he can't swim, one said. *He really does know how to do only one thing!*

Well, a man who couldn't paddle couldn't be much of a threat. The women dove into the water and began pulling his canoe to safety. Their wavy hair glistened in his magnificent light. Their skin was slick and their strong thighs scissored the water. Moon's spiny little fingers danced. He dipped down and tickled the woman on his right.

She immediately told him to stop. His fingers danced along her ribs. She splashed him with water and threatened to call the elders down on him. He didn't care. He hoped to seduce them both by the time they reached the other side.

The women had other plans. When the canoe floated into the strongest part of the current, both women moved to the same side. As they reached up, Moon's heart swelled.

Oh, my beauties, he crooned and leaned over to embrace them.

At just the right moment, the pair pulled down on the hull. The canoe tipped and the cold water swallowed up that gleaming body and those spindly legs. By the time Moon hauled himself out, the women had gone back to their camp.

When he realized how disrespectful he'd been, he felt ashamed. For a long time he didn't go out at all. As he grew bolder, he took longer and longer walks. Even when he slicked up his body to show off that gorgeous gleam, though, women turned away. Then he remembered his shame and hid for a while before peeking out again.

The Message of The Glow

How men and women are expected to act toward each other is an important part of every culture. Because Aboriginal tribes were spread out across Australia's harsh interior, potential mates were often available only when different clans got together. A code of behavior guarded against inbreeding while encouraging long-term pair bonds with appropriate partners.

In the past, our society's codes gave each gender prescribed rules to govern their conduct. We had our own division of labor based on gender (and even on race); women were the primary caregivers for children and parents; and the traditionally male workplace was integrated only when wars drained the supply of able-bodied men.

Opening doors for women or expecting a woman to blush when she receives attention simply doesn't fit today's lifestyles. Making women wait for a man's help and encouraging men to seek out only shy, submissive wives serves neither individual citizens nor the larger society. But the concepts at the core of these customs were based on respect. That's why vestiges of old-fashioned codes still exist.

Women are no longer so hampered by corsets and hoops that they need doors opened for them yet the gesture survives as one of respect. Men are no longer forced to suppress their emotions yet their ability to be a family's strength is still honored. Although restrictions on speech have loosened, adults still frown on foul language as a way to preserve their image...that is, out of respect for themselves.

Too often change, and especially change in behavioral codes, is assumed to mean that good values are being lost. Actually, change is often driven by the core value itself. Nowadays men and women hold doors open for each other as well as for seniors. Dads stay home while moms track down the paycheck. Immodest jokes are restricted to comedies (where we can relieve our usual social stress over such language through laughter) and private functions (where close friends understand that a risqué joke is not a sign of moral decay).

Our modern society recognizes that women and men are individuals. Each has their own set of skills, likes and needs. Only some are naturally shy or in need of assistance or want to retire at a certain age. The rest want to live out loud...or at whatever other volume they deem appropriate. We arrived at our current state by valuing the contributions individuals can make regardless of gender or age or any other category.

The same respect is signaled by the ancient curse for consorting with Moon. Bearing one child was dangerous enough for the mother, and twins doubled the risk. Today a host of advances make pregnancy much less risky yet we still fear for our women. Rapists target those who live alone. Physical and emotional abuse continues at plague proportions. An American woman's risk of being murdered by a domestic partner increases substantially when she becomes pregnant.

Many of our social ailments spring from a lack of self-respect. The issue is not new and is also included in the Dreamtime tale. Moon clearly had some attractive qualities yet he abandoned his lovers to the darkness. He was too bloated with pride to realize that a talent used only to serve himself was a curse to others. By isolating himself, he kept his fragile self-esteem intact. His ego fed on blurry reflections and a glow produced by thick layers of animal fat. The same lies that tricked inexperienced women also tricked Moon.

Shame finally quelled his ego. Society has evolved beyond this technique and we no longer use shame to influence others' decisions. We simply don't know our neighbors well enough for it to be effective. Guilt, the internalized cousin of shame, works when it has been implanted through the values taught to each individual. In our gentler society, though, even guilt is outdated.

Today we rely entirely on self-respect to control our behavior. Neither shame nor guilt can fully overcome the overblown ego of a person who lacks self-respect and who doesn't respect others. Moon's cycles of shame and lust, remorse and self-importance warn us to avoid the charming enchantments of self-centered, misshapen souls. They also remind us to respect ourselves enough to treat others well.

But what of the punishment? Possibly drowning someone for a tickle might appear harsh yet it was perfectly suited to the circumstances. The response eliminated any benefit Moon might have received from the women's assistance. It shocked him into recognizing the impact of his poor behavior. And while his light was hidden underwater, his glow could not seduce anyone else.

In assessing the women's actions, we must remember that a harmless touch can quickly escalate to force or even violence...especially with someone like Moon. The punishment mirrored his crime because it was also a harmless act with the potential to escalate. Today one in three women will be sexually assaulted in her lifetime. Many of those attacks begin with seemingly harmless overtures. Our lifestyles have changed dramatically. Our hearts, including their dark impulses, have not.

People like Moon will always be around. And there will always be people who fall for lies, who blind themselves to spiritual deformities and disregard the warnings of wiser adults. When these individuals tempt danger and escape, when they carry the burden of a curse or heal from heartbreak, they develop self-respect. With that light firing their soul, their glow is more beautiful than that of the moon.

The Promise

All living things slow down as they age. Eventually birds and fish, humans and animals slow down so much that they stop moving. Since the day Creator first touched the Earth, death was the natural endpoint of every life. Then a young cockatoo with plenty of time left fell from a tree. Just like that, he moved no more.

His family tried to coax life back into his body. They bent his legs and folded his wings; they put food on his tongue and massaged his throat until water slipped down to his stomach. Nothing helped. He had been starting a lifetime of days one moment and was as still as an elder who'd completed his years the next. Where had Cockatoo's energy gone?

Magpie said they had never known. Life always ran out like water evaporating from a billabong. Rain filled the pond again but it was new water. The old had been used up.

I disagree, Kangaroo said. *If I drop a stone into water, it sinks out of sight but it still exists. Our energy goes to a place we can neither see nor understand.*

Emu shook his head. He compared life to a stick swept away in monsoon floods. It always washed up later in some other place.

Maybe it doesn't look like a stick anymore, he said. *But life is so strong it has to continue in some form.*

For days the animals argued but no one had an answer. Eagle had never seen anything high above that could end the debate. Crocodiles had never found the truth in the deepest water. Echidnas and bats said that no secrets hid underground, and galahs who nested in hollow tree trunks couldn't claim any special knowledge.

SEVEN SISTERS

As the arguments grew more heated, the animals split into different camps. Each group clung to its theories as if their lives depended on their own version of the mystery. Soon they couldn't talk to each other without shouting, and each group tried to force the others to change their beliefs. They all grew bitter and miserable.

One night the groups stayed locked in debate until morning. As dawn broke, the shouting reached a peak. Kangaroo and Emu were ready to tear each other apart. Their followers watched eagerly, hoping that a fight would eliminate one enemy. Brute force would prove who was right. Only the giant lizard Goanna tried to stop them.

This is ridiculous! she shouted. *You are both ready to die when you are searching for an answer about life!*

Emu would not back down. The question was important. No one's hearts or minds could be at peace until they knew what lay beyond. If another group believed something different, that meant someone was wrong. The possibility that their own beliefs might be in error caused them terrible pain. Only by silencing others could they silence their own doubts.

Goanna's next words brought them hope. Since the body grew still after death, perhaps staying still would allow the living to discover where the life force went. Goanna would sit in a deep hole where no light or sound could distract her. If she stayed still long enough, she might find the truth.

Emu and Kangaroo agreed to postpone their fight until after her experiment. The lizard disappeared inside her burrow for many weeks. When she finally emerged, she had to drink deeply from the billabong before she could speak. *I saw nothing,* she croaked. *I do not know the answer.*

The animals abandoned their questions. The dry season had come and they had no time for anything but survival. After a long, hard drought, the rains returned. Blankets of wildflowers sprang up and frogs clogged the waterholes with eggs. Budgies gathered at the billabongs and their chatter drew the animals together again.

Then the insects emerged. Pale grubs had become glossy beetles with iridescent armor. Locust nymphs split their shells and screamed their deafening songs. Shapeless caterpillars had become butterflies dancing on dusted wings. Kangaroo stared at them for a very long while. Then she said, *We should have known.*

The insects showed them Creator's promise. Every living thing, no matter when or how it stopped moving, would eventually be born anew. Each spring, Creator again sends proof of this divine truth through the most humble of creatures.

The Message of The Promise

So often when we explore traditional stories, we assume that a culture's beliefs were static and unchanging. Really, though, neither rigorous memorization nor a written language can keep the human mind from adapting. A question that hasn't been asked before is still important. People who live one way for generations can embrace new ideas.

The process can be painful. People question truths old and new; they question one another and their place in the world. They collect in groups to congratulate each other on being right. Within those enclaves, the strict interpretation of their system grows more ossified. Out of a deep concern for their fellow humans, they force their beliefs on opposing camps. Sound familiar?

Funny, though. In this story, all the theories were right. Creatures do die, and new animals and plants and people spring from the same material but are not the same being that died. All life is animated by the same type of energy, an individual consciousness that is nevertheless connected to God, Creator, the Cosmic One. The life force really is like rain that fills up the billabongs: it is not exactly the same water that evaporated but it all flows from the same source.

The idea that life goes to a place we cannot know or understand is also true. Even people who've undergone near-death experiences have seen only a waiting room for what lies beyond. We see our ancestors there because our memory preserves a certain energy pattern. They are present for that person yet their form doesn't match anything in the material plane. If we can accept what physics tells us about a particle's ability to exist in multiple locations at once, we know that a spirit can exist in the astral plane and its next incarnation in the same moment.

The concept that all or part of a specific life force returns to the material plane is also true. Since we are all connected, parts of us have lived before and parts of us will live again. When we die, our individual energy blends with the cosmic energy. A tiny part of it returns to Earth while the rest takes up other adventures throughout the universe.

It doesn't matter if you believe all, one or none of these concepts. When we began exploring these ancient stories, we understood that while the details of culture and environment would be different, the issues would be universally human. Beliefs about the afterlife are merely a patina around core truths: a specific energy animates life; we can access the divine because it is around us and within us; we are at once perfect and striving for perfection.

The animals' debate reflects our natural tendency to question and discover...and to become burdened by fear. They feared that holding incorrect beliefs would prevent them from entering the next life. They feared that loved ones who believed differently would be separated from them for eternity. They feared, finally, that fewer people in their group meant their own beliefs might be wrong.

We cannot be enlightened if we are burdened by fear. Panic blinds the seeker; desperation spins into war. Fear of the divine or of the divine self prevents people from approaching even their own god. Fear of other beliefs, even when the details are only minutely different, is the fear of death. And fearing death leads to the fear of living fully, of risking cherished beliefs and the community of like-minded believers even when change would enhance our spirits and our lives.

We become lost in the details. Like the animals we ask, *Stick or stone? Light or dark? Created or evolved? Limited or eternal?* If we would just open our hearts, we would discover that we already know the answer. Creator—the energy, the intent, the God, the godhead; again, the details of its name or its form don't matter—has promised rebirth. Partial or complete, in this world or another, even as an entirely different kind of energy, all life will be born anew.

Before the animals could achieve this new level of understanding, they had to create peace. It is good to debate and exchange ideas. But we must not do battle for our beliefs. That only harms our friends. No matter who is victorious, spiritual wars provide no answers.

Goanna provided an alternative. She dedicated herself to ascetic meditation for as long as her body could bear. She was already good at physical stillness; by applying that same discipline in an isolated state, she achieved mental stillness. Although she failed to produce an answer, her effort created peace.

In accepting this peace, the animals surrendered. Not to each other but to the contest that fed their fear. Why kill for a personal image of heaven when surviving in physical form was difficult enough? When they released anxiety and stress and fear, they opened themselves to the truth.

If we open ourselves to the divine touch and the humble whispers, we will hear the messages that surround us. When we release our expectations about this stick or that stone, details no longer limit us. Instead we rise with the waters and touch the cosmic one. We mingle in the mist and gather bits of information like dew. Then we return with another piece of the universal truth that is the birthright of our planet.

No single answer will satisfy everyone. We are not intended to all be happy with the same system, the same perspective or the same cycle of seasons. When we share the messages we have received personally, belief will spark in certain listeners...perhaps thousands, perhaps only one. Numbers do not matter. It matters only how the message resonates within our hearts.

Any attempt to force others to accept a certain belief makes everyone bitter and miserable. We need not fight over the afterlife when we live our current lives fully. We should discuss it, yes. We should prepare ourselves for death and help others transition; these are sacred duties we owe each other. But the moment we declare war, we fight not for concepts or souls or even for the details but only out of fear.

Despite our differences, we are all divine. Let our new stories, the ones that spring from our modern lives, resonate with this holy truth. May we live in peace with love for all.

A Final Message

Our journey through the outback has ended. Our journey through the eternal Dreamtime continues. These stories and essays are guideposts to which you can return for support. You will likely find their messages repeated at new points along your Dreaming, and each new reading will take you deeper into their truths. You will surely begin to hear messages from your own ancestor spirits and the cosmic one.

This is my passion, to help you access the messages intended only for you. By listening deeply to your own higher self, you will discover that ancient connection to god/goddess/the divine that has been with you since consciousness manifested.

May your relationship with the All-knowing Force lead you to your personal truth. May the light of your own perfection illuminate your heart path. May you hold it or share it as you see fit. No matter what you choose, know that your divine beauty and your radiant soul support all living things.

From the Heart of Love,
Laine Cunningham

A free sample from

Woman Alone
A Six-Month Journey Through the Australian Outback

Introduction

SOME YEARS AGO, I did something that most people, depending on their taste for risk, might consider daring, adventurous, or idiotic. I chucked everything to spend six months camping—alone, as a woman—in the Australian Outback.

Sounds bold, maybe, unless you know that the life I had constructed stick by stick and day by day was empty. The college degree that suited my goals as a novelist left me unsuited to a wide range of income-producing options, so I had landed in a corporate job I utterly despised.

My depression wasn't clinical—I functioned well enough and held down a job and ate regularly and exercised—but I was anything except happy. Every morning I dragged myself into an office building where my peers viciously tore down the overweight woman on our team, invented horribly clever and horribly misogynistic nicknames for our boss (most of my peers were women), and gossiped endlessly about who was sleeping with whom and what that might mean for the woman's career advancement (never the man's).

I lived in a basement apartment with so many health and safety violations that the police officer who arrived when my car was broken into offered to report my landlord. I declined because

I would have been forced to find another place I could afford, a tall order in the Washington, DC metropolitan area.

I had tons of friends and went out nearly every weekend but the bar scene and the punk rock scene and the all-night party/hookup scene and the hanging out at movie night getting stoned scene had grown stale even before I'd received my degree. I had already dedicated myself to becoming a writer but was too mentally exhausted to get much writing done.

And that was the real problem. Because I wasn't pursuing my true place in the world, the life I was leading—corporatized, industrialized, and in which everything I had ever been taught to want had been falsely glamorized—was killing me.

Something had to be done. What, I wasn't exactly sure. For a year, I reached out to my company's London office. My father's family is at least half Scotts-Irish, so the transfer would have opened up explorations into that side of my heritage.

By the time the foreign office's director made it clear—through a blunt, face-to-face conversation that materialized only because we both happened to arrive at the deserted Virginia office at six in the morning—that an offer would never be extended, my backup plan had already been funded with a fat savings account.

The idea was to knock around in the UK until the money ran out. I hoped to be there for a year but the expenses made it much more likely I would only wander for six months. I would see the sights, visit the rolling countryside, and work on losing as much of my tan as any self-respecting UK citizen. Who knew what might arise during that time? Where might I land?

I applied for a sabbatical and started packing. Anything I wouldn't truly need when…if…I returned to the US was sold off or given away. The rest was stored in my parents' basement. Even the car I had so lovingly restored, and into which I had sunk a feverish amount of money, was put up for sale. The Triumph was too temperamental to sit unattended for six hours let alone six months, so selling it was the best option.

As the final sixty days ticked away, something bizarre and unsettling happened. Time and again, I was visited by vivid dreams of kangaroos and the red desert. Over the course of a few weeks, the images went from foggy to sharply intense.

These dream-visions never came when I was deeply asleep. Instead they appeared like beautiful hallucinations whenever I was drowsing. Their gravitational pull caught at my heart. As I rose up out of each one, its threads and its images clung to me for minutes and then hours.

Finally I surrendered. All right, already! I'll go to Australia!

I knew nothing about the country or what I might do there. But one thing was clear: this journey I had decided to take had always been about the Outback...even before I'd started dreaming.

That was perfectly fine with me. I'd considered hiking through America's largest national parks for a year but I really wanted to leave the country. Rather than walk the UK's cliffs and moors, perhaps I could camp in the desert.

No matter how I spent my time in Australia, though, something was waiting for me. Something had grown tired of waiting and was reaching out. I bought the ticket.

The frenzied preparations that went with switching destinations began. My division head had already said the company would not guarantee that my position would be open when I returned. In my mind, there was no guarantee that I would return to that company or even to the US.

With less than two weeks to go, I took a nap on the couch. As I drifted closer toward sleep, I fell into a vision of astonishing clarity. My spirit soared over red desert plains where a few stunted trees dotted the broad earth. I swooped down toward a lone tree with a twisted black trunk. Its thin canopy cast jagged shadows over a corpse.

My corpse. I floated inches above it, peering at the face to be certain that it was me and that I was dead. A film of dust coated eyes that stared blankly at the sky.

The shock jolted me awake. I sat for a long time thinking about how clear and detailed the vision had been. Was this a warning? I was twenty-seven years old. Any trip a woman undertakes alone involves risks, and wandering through undeveloped regions in a foreign country would entail dangers of which I was ignorant. This wasn't supposed to be a suicide mission. Should I cancel the trip?

In a way, though, I was already dead. Returning to the life I had been living was unthinkable. The depression that weighed me down, the sheer grind of sameness at my job, the poisonous gossip and the stretch of similar days would never end unless something was done…done by me, and done for me.

I decided to go. Even if I died in the outback, for a few short months—and really for the first time in my life—I would have lived fully.

I told no one about the vision. Too many opinions had already been proffered about my plans. My parents were of course worried but knew it was hopeless to try to dissuade me. My friends thought it was great while pointing out the homes, children, and responsibilities that prevented them from undertaking the same type of journey. My department head didn't think I'd last more than two months before begging for my job back. Who would I tell?

Halfway through the journey, I would find that lonely, twisted tree. The events that would take place there would threaten my life and be entirely out of my control…until, that is, I made a choice.

A choice made by me. A choice made for me.

That experience and my choice would change me forever. After finding that tree, the rest of my time in the Outback would be different. It would feel less compelling, as if marking that milepost had accomplished everything I'd come to achieve.

Eventually I realized that it had marked the turning point I'd hoped to find. My life before that tree had been so flawed that the escape hatch had been hidden. Still I'd known, or my heart had known, that a new road would lead to more than just surviving in a salaried position, more than just getting through every day by keeping my head down and my mouth shut.

Only a dramatic and dangerous event could reveal that road. Only facing death allowed me to choose life.

Before I headed into the Outback, the many people who had confessed that they wanted to do something similar also said that their kids, their spouse, their mortgage, their whatever were insurmountable obstacles that prevented them from undertaking their own journeys.

The truth is that they were also making a choice. They were bypassing one dream in order to pursue or maintain a different dream they valued more. Before my sabbatical, I purged nearly all my material possessions. That left the entire world open to possibility...even the possibility that my life would end.

Not everyone can or should take such drastic steps. But people who allow other considerations to overshadow their dreams should let go of the vision or idea or concept that actually isn't their dream. Stability, raising a family, and cultivating a life that's filled with comfort and joy are all dreams that can be fulfilled...if the dreamers are willing to make conscious and informed choices.

No matter what your dream looks like, my wish is that the book you're holding right now provides the hope and inspiration to launch you onto your own path. In these pages, you'll find the usual traveler's stories brightly painted with the ways other people live. You'll read some of my comments and hear the thoughts of others. Along the way, perhaps you'll find an undiscovered part of yourself. Perhaps you'll mark your own milestone.

Turn the page with every hope for the person you can become.

You've just finished reading a free sample from
Woman Alone
A Six-Month Journey Through the Australian Outback

A free sample from

The Family Made of Dust

A Novel of Loss and Rebirth in the Australian Outback

1 The Precious Dead

WHEN A MAN DIES IN THE DESERT, he is completely alone. At thirty-nine, Ian McCabe knew this simple fact. He had spent most of his life working the demanding seasonal jobs that kept Australia's rural towns alive. He had seen a flat tire turn deadly, and knew that beauty and danger were the sisters who bore the land.

Ian was not a tall man but a shock of blond hair added inches to his height. Quick blue eyes and a steady aim were useful in his career as a kangaroo culler. Every night the slim .22 found its target between the shine of an animal's eyes. On cattle stations hundreds of kilometers wide, engine trouble and the bite of the brown snake posed constant threats.

Ian's white Land Rover was nearly twenty years old and it still ran like a lizard drinking—non-stop and practically unstoppable. In the rear a skillet, bedroll and a case of green beans were strapped onto narrow shelves. A bottle of port nestled in its own padded compartment, and a few golf clubs were tied to the wall. Sleep, slurp and sport, he called the collection, everything a man could want in one mobile space.

He eased the truck down the track. The spur was rough, really a strip of earth scraped clean of boulders, but it saved nearly half an hour. Besides, the less traveled a road was, the happier Ian felt. Cities, he knew, were for suckers. Why squeeze into a rabbit hutch when the outback was right next door?

This area, so close to the Davenport Ranges, was typical of the Northern Territory. Wide plains of twisted mulga trees reached southwest to Alice Springs. A network of creeks and rivers that ran only during the Wet sustained gum trees taller than most buildings. Cockatoos raised their young in the hollow trunks, and after a rain lorikeets gorged on the nectar in the blossoms.

Grass was sparse, edged out by the ubiquitous spinifex that cut flesh as cruelly as broken glass. Only the toughest creatures survived and half-feral Brahma cattle were the breed of choice. To a rancher beleaguered by drought and debt, every blade eaten by native animals robbed them of beef. Roo shooters were always welcome. And judging by the sun, Ian would arrive at the station house in time for dinner.

A flash of metal caught his eye. Through binoculars, he watched a red SUV beetle across the property. The truck stayed behind the ridges and moved slowly enough to keep its dust cloud low. The same stealth kept Ian from sight as he followed.

Eventually the trespassers parked beside a hill topped by a stone pinnacle. Ian stuffed the Land Rover under a mulga tree and watched as a pair of men hiked up the slope. The first, a sturdy white fellow about thirty years old, clutched a rifle. His legs were bowed so severely he rocked as he mounted the boulders.

The other man, an Aborigine who might have been in his sixties, moved steadily upward. He was wiry yet had the grace of a predator. The outback was filled with men like them, drifters who found the bush far removed from the law.

At the top, the elder found a cleft in the rock. From this cache he retrieved a board nearly as long as his arm. Ian had seen dancers perform with similar objects and knew they were supposed to be magical. The cubby surrendered perhaps a dozen other artifacts. All would fetch a small fortune on the black market.

While the older man worked steadily, the bowlegged bloke couldn't keep a proper watch. First he rubbed his nose with the back of his arm. Then he adjusted his shorts. He scanned the landscape, rifle at ready. Then he swatted a fly. Rubbed sweat through his hair. Tugged at his crotch. Abruptly he was alert again, scowling while the gun grew hot in the sun.

As they retreated, the Aborigine erased his footprints with a leafy branch. Ian let the SUV jangle out of sight before picking up the trail. They traveled faster now and corkscrewed across their original path. Where the spur intersected a paved road dusty tread marks headed toward the Stuart Highway, the only paved north-south road through the Territory. The pair could pick from dozens of unmarked byways. The artifacts would disappear.

Ian pushed the Land Rover to its limit. Although the old truck handled beautifully in the bush, it was as sluggish as a fly in winter. The needle was still climbing when Ian saw the red SUV parked beside the highway. If he pulled over, the men would surely notice when he followed them later.

The Toyota, a new model free of dents or scrapes, faced the road. The younger man smirked and the lines around his mouth twisted. Again Ian was struck by the elder's expression. White pipe clay severed his forehead and chin, and his face was a jigsaw of violence.

"So you've seen me," Ian murmured, "and I've seen you." He adjusted the rearview mirror but couldn't make out the tag number.

A roadhouse a quarter-hour away was a convenient place to watch for the men but they never appeared. It was possible they had turned east toward the coast. More likely they had dodged off into the bush. As night covered the sky, Ian had plenty of time to consider his next action.

He didn't need a fraction of it. The kangaroos could wait.

Thousands of kilometers to the east, Gabriel Branch loaded the last of his bags into the hatchback. At six feet tall, Gabe barely fit behind the wheel even with the seat pushed all the way back. But the rear compartment was roomy enough to hold all his diving gear, and the hatch was easier to use than a station wagon. He squeezed in and steered for the coastal highway out of Townsville.

The next few days would be spent an hour or so south on the Whitsunday Islands. In the forty-five years Gabe had lived in Queensland, he rarely traveled more than a hundred kilometers inland. The neighbors never quite understood why his vacations didn't take advantage of the expansive desert at their back doors.

They didn't understand the...complications of Gabe's life. Oh, they knew about the Aboriginal land rights issues that had consumed the media for decades, and had heard about the children adopted by white families in a long-defunct effort to assimilate the race. But they didn't know what it was like to be caught by those issues against their will. Only a biracial Aborigine who had been assimilated at the age of three could tell them that. And Gabe wasn't talking.

Nor was he interested in drawing attention. Black faces were scarce in Australia, so he stuck close to the coastal cities that hosted international travelers in all their rainbow colors. He blended in better there and no one asked many questions about his background. Even when they did, they were met with silence.

Silence had kept his life on the smooth, orderly track he worked so hard to create. Last week he had hit a bump—a big bump—in his relationship with a Jamaican woman. Chance hadn't been in the country more than a few years. But she had some definite ideas about how much Gabe should say about his experiences and how loudly his voice should sound.

They had fought about it more of late. He supposed it was the same with all couples, as if money or household chores or work schedules were the cause of their problems instead of a symptom. Whatever the real reason, Gabe and Chance had split up last week. The separation was supposedly temporary, just a little breathing and thinking room, but Gabe knew where that would lead.

If Ian had been available, Gabe would have talked things over with him. In fifteen years of friendship, the men had seen each other through a number of breakups. None had been as serious as this one, though, and Gabe wished Ian would call. He already missed Chance's rapid-fire commentary and her odd machinegun laugh. Before the split, Gabe had been thinking of proposing. But courage in one person required courage in the other. And that, he knew, was the real reason their separation would be permanent.

When Ian did call, Gabe was already out of range. He heard only the clack of sugar cane as he sped past the coastal farms.

Ian tracked the men for days without coming within twenty kilometers of the truck. The outback was so big and its population so small, a little luck and a few calls let him keep tabs on the thieves as they passed through different roadhouses. At a tourist site called Devil's Marbles, a vendor remembered the odd pair and pointed to a faint track heading west.

When he located the Toyota, he parked some distance away and hiked in for a better look. Perhaps a dozen coffins had been removed from crevices in a wadi. The thieves were stealing bodies. Ian trotted back to the Land Rover and gunned the engine, all but honking to make sure they heard as he rattled toward the ridge.

The thieves took the hint. After the Toyota disappeared, Ian walked into the gully to inspect the damage. The coffins, each a cradle for the precious dead, were lined up in the center. Tarps and coils of rope had been left behind, along with cigarette butts and candy wrappers. The urine drying on the cliff face still smelled sharp.

Then Ian spotted the truck tucked under a ledge. It was the same one he had seen leave, he was sure of it. The guano he had noticed days earlier was still smeared on the side window. Yet the culvert had no other entrance except the one he had just walked through.

A bullet spun him off his feet. He heard nothing, not even the echo of the shot, as his shirt soaked in a red tide. The blood was brilliant at first, like the eyes of the metallic starlings that congregated around his boyhood home. He saw the Aborigine kneel beside him as his breath fled past his tongue.

The man was older than he had thought, much older, and carried with him the aura of ancient things. He wore only a string belt, a pair of shorts, and bands on his arms and legs. Tufts of cockatoo feathers framed a radiant face. On his chest a swirl of dots and circles, made hypnotic by his breath, pulled Ian into a galaxy of red.

He was terribly confused. He tried to separate the ringing in his head from his memories. *They ran away,* he thought. He had *seen* them drive across the plateau that drained west of the escarpment, had watched them until they were out of sight. The tire tracks he had crossed floated in his mind. Only one set of tracks, he realized. The truck had never left. How could he have been so wrong?

As if to offer comfort, the elder caressed Ian's forehead. The man's hair, shot with gray, looked nutmeg. It was as if his great age had worn the shine off the strands and leached away the pigment. His eyes were luminous, though, beyond the touch of time. Ian thought of the dingoes that gazed into his spotlight. The dogs always waited, knowing he would leave the kangaroo's heart and liver and kidneys for their feast.

Suddenly he understood. This man was a shaman. Ian had been lured into the culvert just as he had been tricked into speeding down the highway. He smiled and reached up.

"There, now," the man soothed, and flicked his blade across Ian's throat.

You've just finished reading a free sample from
The Family Made of Dust
A Novel of Loss and Rebirth in the Australian Outback

About the Author

After Laine Cunningham's first novel won two national awards, she enjoyed a ten-year relationship with a leading literary agent. Jack Scovil of Scovil Galen Ghosh worked with Norman Mailer, Carl Sagan, Morris West, and Arthur C. Clark. He represented two additional novels from Laine before his death in 2012.

All Laine's novels interweave social, cultural, historical, political and spiritual movements that have occurred within different groups and at different time periods. These elements are intended to engage modern readers in discussions of how similar forces have changed or are changing the contemporary world...and what might lie in our own future.

The end result hopefully engages not just debate but action. When individuals recognize how large issues build over time from multiple small steps, many of which were taken up by individuals just like them, they recognize that everyone can foment change through their choices and their decisions.

Laine's tenure in publishing spans twenty years and encompasses ghostwriting and pitching for other authors. That expansive experience fuels her efforts to reverse engineer the publishing industry. Her first step is *Writing While Female or Black or Gay: Diverse Voices in Publishing*. The book is available in print and electronic editions.

Laine's first novel, *The Family Made of Dust: A Novel of Loss and Rebirth in the Australian Outback*, is a work of literary suspense based on the Australian government's assimilation policy. Until early in the 1970s, biracial and light-skinned Aboriginal children were forcibly removed from their parents. In the novel, Gabriel Branch searches the outback for his best friend and stumbles on an artifact smuggling ring...and the Aboriginal heritage he lost as a child. *The Family Made of Dust* was called "the best novel in ten years" by the Hackney Literary Award committee. The James Jones Literary Society said it "demonstrates a mastery of psychological introspection and an uncanny feel for the spirit of place."

Her second novel, *Beloved: A Noir Thriller,* follows an Indian-American FBI agent who sees visions from *The Ramayana,* a Hindu epic of good versus evil. Priya was led to law enforcement because she is the product of a gang-rape that occurred in India. While tracking a sadistic sexual predator, she accesses the dark powers of the goddess Kali. *Beloved* was supported by two residencies and one grant; it was shortlisted for three national awards.

Reparation is Laine's most recent work. Aidan Little Boy, a Lakota Sioux man, must stop the leader of a Native American-style peyote church before he enacts the largest mass murder ever to take place on US soil. *Reparation* was shortlisted for three national awards and has been compared to Terence Malick's *The New World.*

www.LaineCunningham.com

www.WritersResource.us

Other Works by Laine Cunningham

Fiction

The Family Made of Dust
A Novel of Loss and Rebirth in the Australian Outback
When Gabriel Branch searches the outback for his best friend, he crosses paths with a tribal shaman who forces him to face the Aboriginal heritage he lost as a child.
Winner of two national awards.

Beloved
A Noir Thriller
A female FBI agent must access the dark power of the Hindu goddess Kali to bring a serial killer to justice.
Recipient of one arts grant.
Supported by two arts residencies.

Reparation
A short vacation turns into a sinister game to save a sister from a peyote cult in this compulsive and compelling story about a Native American man.
Shortlisted for three national awards.

Nonfiction

Writing While Female or Black or Gay
Diverse Voices in Publishing
A twenty-year publishing professional's insights into the lack of diversity in publishing.

Woman Alone
A Six-Month Journey Through the Australian Outback

THE *WOMAN ALONE* COMPANION SERIES

18,000 Miles
An Australia Travel Guide Companion to Woman Alone

Amazing Australia
A Traveler's Guide to Common Plants and Animals

On the Wallaby Track
Essential Australian Word and Phrases

Fairy Bread and Bush Tucker
Surviving Gastronomical Adventures in Australia (With Recipes)

THE ZEN FOR LIFE SERIES

The Zen of Travel
Wisdom from the Journey

The Zen of Gardening
Wisdom Rooted in the Earth

Zen in the Stable
Wisdom from the Equestrian Life

The Zen of Chocolate
Wisdom by the Bar

The Zen of Dogs
Wisdom That Wags the Tail

THE WISDOM FOR LIFE SERIES

The Wisdom of Puppies
Puppyhood as a Life Path

The Wisdom of Babies
Life Lessons from the Diaper Set

The Wisdom of Weddings
Life Lessons From That Special Day

THE TRAVEL PHOTO ART SERIES

Bikes of Berlin
Necropolises of New Orleans I & II
Ruins of Rome
Ancients of Assisi
Panoramas of Portugal

www.ingramcontent.com/pod-product-compliance
Lightning Source LLC
Chambersburg PA
CBHW041302240426
43661CB00010B/996